Contents

COOKERY NOTES

- Both metric and imperial measures are given for the recipes. Follow either metric or imperial throughout as they are not interchangeable.
- All spoon measures are level unless otherwise stated. Sets of measuring spoons are available in both metric and imperial sizes for accurate measurement of small quantities.
- Ovens should be preheated to the specified temperature. Grills should also be preheated. The cooking times given in the recipes assume that this has been done.

- If a stage is specified under freezing instructions, the dish should be frozen at the end of that stage.
- Size 2 eggs should be used except where otherwise specified. Free-range eggs are recommended.
- Use freshly ground black pepper unless otherwise specified.
- Use fresh rather than dried herbs unless dried herbs are suggested in the recipe.
- Always use freshly grated or shredded Parmesan, not ready-grated cheese.

INTRODUCTION

Chicken is one of our most popular foods. Its versatility makes it suitable for most occasions from the humblest weekday supper to the smartest celebration meal. It is also full of protein and B vitamins and, once the skin is trimmed away, it has a very low fat content – making it ideal from a nutritional angle, too.

One potential disadvantage is the intensive methods used to rear the majority of chickens sold in this country. Apart from the inhumanity of this, there's no doubt that the combination of a grain diet and the freedom to wander in the open air produces the best flavour. More and more consumers are becoming aware of the advantages of free-range poultry and virtually all supermarkets and most butchers now stock a variety of free-range birds. They're well worth the extra expense.

CHOOSING POULTRY

Choose a free-range bird in preference. Obviously the bird should be as fresh as possible, so if buying from a supermarket check the use-by date. Look for a good plump breast with a firm unblemished skin. If buying from a farm, refuse a bird that's been carelessly plucked and singed. A young chicken will have a pliable breastbone, and a young duckling a pliable beak.

STORAGE

All poultry contains low levels of salmonella and campylobacter – the bacteria which can cause food poisoning if they multiply. It is therefore important that it is handled and stored hygienically. Always get poultry home and into a fridge as soon as possible after buying. If the bird contains giblets take them out and store in a separate container, since these will deteriorate most rapidly.

Always wash your hands before and after handling poultry – and never use the same utensils for preparing raw poultry and cooked foods. It's a good idea to keep one chopping board specifically for preparing raw poultry. Pay particular attention to cleaning knives, chopping boards and work surfaces. If you have a dishwasher put plastic boards and knives through a hot cycle, or scrub thoroughly in plenty of very hot soapy water.

FROZEN POULTRY

Frozen poultry will keep for up to 3 months. Make sure that it is well wrapped to prevent the delicate skin from being damaged by freezer burn. Ensure that frozen poultry is fully thawed before cooking. The current view is that it should be thawed at cool room temperature rather than in the refrigerator.

If necessary poultry can be thawed in the microwave, using the defrost setting, but you will need to watch carefully as thinner or exposed parts may begin to cook. This is most likely to be a problem with large birds that can appear to be thawed but may still contain ice crystals in the centre. A thawed bird will be flexible – try moving the leg joints.

Once fully thawed, poultry can be stored in the refrigerator for a short time but is best cooked as soon as possible. If it has been thawed in the microwave it should be cooked straight away.

CUTS OF CHICKEN AND OTHER POULTRY

Because chicken is so popular, manufacturers are constantly developing new cuts to tempt us. In addition to the familiar quarters, breast fillets, thighs and drumsticks, there is a wide variety of other cuts readily available. Look out for thin strips of breast meat called goujons, suitable for stir-frying or coating in egg and breadcrumbs and deep-frying; turkey steaks and chops for grilling or barbecuing; turkey escalopes (cut from the breast) for stir-frying or rolling and stuffing; as well as chicken and turkey mince. Skinned and flattened chicken breast fillets are known as escalopes, and breast fillets sold with the wing bone attached are called supremes.

Similar cuts of chicken and turkey are interchangeable – so if a recipe calls for tender chicken breast meat, turkey fillet or escalopes could be substituted. Slow cooked casseroles, curries and stews containing chicken drumsticks or thighs could be made with turkey leg meat instead.

Corn-fed chickens have a distinctive yellow colour and characteristic flavour because they are reared on a diet of maize. Guinea fowl are lean golden birds with a superb flavour. Both corn-fed chickens and guinea fowl are cooked in the same way as chickens. Poussins are 4-6 week old chickens, weighing 450-675 g (1-1½ lb). One poussin serves one or two people.

DUCKLING

Whole ducklings are available fresh and frozen, and duckling portions are now much easier to come by too. Duckling breasts are solid meat with a good layer of fat that should be cooked until crisp. They usually weigh around 225 g (8 oz) each, making a generous serving for one. If you buy the larger 350 g (12 oz) *magret* size, one should serve two people. Unless cooked in a casserole, duckling breasts are at their best served crisp and browned on the outside while retaining a hint of pink in the centre.

Wild duck has a stronger more gamey flavour than its farm-reared counterpart. It can be treated in the same way. If using wild duckling joints you may find that the meat is very bloody (particularly if you've jointed it at home). To remove excess blood, soak the joints in cold water for an hour before cooking.

ROASTING CHICKEN

Allow at least 350 g (12 oz) per person. Remove the giblets and use for making gravy. If you're stuffing a whole bird, put the stuffing in the neck end only. If you stuff the body cavity it slows down the heat penetration and means there's more chance of an undercooked result, with potential health risks. Don't pack the stuffing too tight, as it will expand on cooking and you don't want the skin to split or the stuffing to ooze out. Cook any excess separately in a small dish.

If you don't want stuffing, put half a lemon, a few fresh herbs and a few peeled garlic cloves in the body cavity for flavour.

At this stage, it's a good idea to truss the bird so that it keeps its shape (see page 7). If you haven't the inclination for trussing, simply fold the wings under the body, then tie the legs together with a piece of string or secure with a skewer or cocktail sticks.

Weigh the whole bird and calculate the cooking time, allowing 20 minutes per 450 g (1 lb) plus 20 minutes. Put the bird in a roasting tin, season with salt and pepper and smear the breast with butter or oil or cover with a few rashers of fatty bacon.

Roast in a preheated oven at 200°C (400°F) Mark 6 for the calculated time or until the juices run clear when the thickest part of the thigh is pierced with a skewer or fork. Baste with the accumulated juices from time to time during roasting to keep the meat moist. If the breast shows signs of browning too quickly, cover it with a piece of foil.

Chicken portions can be roasted at the same temperature and will take about 30-45 minutes depending on their size. Poussins will take 45 minutes to 1 hour, depending on size. Like a whole chicken, the juices will run clear when cooked.

ROASTING TURKEY

Allow at least 300 g (10 oz) per person (see the chart overleaf). Like chickens, turkeys should be stuffed in the neck end only to ensure rapid heat penetration. Stuff just before cooking.

Weigh the stuffed bird and calculate the cooking time allowing for 20 minutes' resting time before carving (this makes the bird easier to carve). Season, then smear with butter or oil as above. Wrap loosely in foil or put the turkey straight into a deep roasting tin. Roast in a preheated oven at 180°C (350°F) Mark 4 for the time suggested (in the chart overleaf), basting frequently to keep the bird moist. Fold back the foil about 45 minutes before the end of the calculated cooking time to brown and crisp the breast. Test as above.

TURKEY ROASTING CHART

OVEN-READY WEIGHT ❖	THAWING TIME (AT ROOM TEMPERATURE) ❖	NUMBER OF SERVINGS ❖	COOKING FOIL-WRAPPED ❖	COOKING WITHOUT FOIL ❖
575 g–1.4 kg (1¼–3 lb)	4–10 hr	2–4	1¾–2 hr	1½–1¾ hr
1.4–2.3 kg (3–5 lb)	10–15 hr	4–6	2–2½ hr	1¾–2 hr
2.3–3.6 kg (5–8 lb)	15–18 hr	6–10	2½–3½ hr	2–2½ hr
3.6–5 kg (8–11 lb)	18–20 hr	10–15	3½–4 hr	2½–3¼ hr
5–6.8 kg (11–15 lb)	20–24 hr	15–20	4–5 hr	3¼–3¾ hr
6.8–9 kg (15–20 lb)	24–30 hr	20–30	5–5½ hr	3¾–4¼ hr
9–11.3 kg (20–25 lb)	30–36 hr	30–40	not recommended	4¼–4¾ hr
11.3–13.5 kg (25–30 lb)	36–48 hr	40–50	not recommended	4¾–5½ hr

ROASTING DUCKLING

Allow at least 450 g (1 lb) per person. Weigh the duckling and calculate the cooking time allowing 30-35 minutes per 450 g (1 lb). Stuffing is best cooked separately. Thoroughly prick the skin and rub with salt. Put the duck on a trivet in a roasting tin and roast in a preheated oven at 180°C (350°F) Mark 4.

If you prefer the breast meat a little pink, remove the duckling from the oven about 30 minutes before the end of the calculated cooking time. Remove the legs and return them to the oven for the remainder of the calculated time. Pierce the breast – the juices should look just pink. Carve the breast and serve. The legs can be served separately.

PEPPER AND RICE STUFFING

Grill 2 peppers until the skins are charred; allow to cool, then peel and chop the flesh. Boil 50 g (2 oz) rice until just tender; drain. Mix with the peppers, 45 ml (3 tbsp) pesto sauce, 2 chopped spring onions and 1 grated courgette. Season well. Add a little beaten egg to bind the stuffing.

LEMON AND PISTACHIO STUFFING

Cook 1 finely chopped onion with 1 crushed garlic clove in 25 g (1 oz) butter until soft. Add 125 g (4 oz) fresh breadcrumbs, 45 ml (3 tbsp) chopped fresh herbs, the finely grated rind of 1 lemon, a squeeze of juice and 25 g (1 oz) pistachio nuts. Season well. Add a little beaten egg to bind everything together.

GRAVY

Use chicken giblets to make a well flavoured stock if they're available. If not, boil up chicken bones and trimmings with plenty of vegetables and a bouquet garni. Alternatively, you could buy concentrated chicken stock from a supermarket, use a can of chicken consommé or resort to a chicken or vegetable stock cube. To impart character, include a little mashed roast garlic (cooked with the bird); a splash of red or white wine (then reduced to evaporate the alcohol); or fragrant herbs like thyme, bay and tarragon.

Roast duck and turkey both have a stronger flavour than chicken so they can take a more robust gravy. A spoonful or two of cranberry, redcurrant or blackcurrant jelly adds a pleasant fruitiness, while a little orange zest or balsamic vinegar can help to offset the richness of duck. Use sherry or madeira rather than wine in a duck gravy. Whole aromatic spices, such as cardamom, coriander, cinnamon and star anise, simmered with the finished gravy, lend a subtle aroma and flavour.

PREPARATION TECHNIQUES

For the recipes in this book, you should be able to buy the particular bird or cut of poultry ready-prepared from your local poulterer, butcher or large supermarket. However, should you prefer to prepare the poultry yourself, the following step-by-step guides will enable you to do so.

TRUSSING POULTRY

Trussing keeps the bird in a neat compact shape for even roasting. It also keeps in the stuffing and makes carving easier. You will need a trussing needle threaded with fine cotton string.

1. Remove giblets. Fold neck skin under body, then fold the wing tips back and under so that they hold it in position. Put the bird on its back and push the legs well into the sides.

2. Push the trussing needle through the second joint of one wing, into the body and out through the corresponding joint on the opposite side.

3. Insert the needle again in the first joint of the wing, pushing it through the flesh at the back of the body (catching the wing tips and the neck skin) and out through the opposite side. You should be back near where you started in step 2. Cut the string. Tie the two ends together.

4. Re-thread the needle. To truss the legs, push the needle in through the gristle at the right side of the parson's nose. Pass string over the right leg, over the left leg, then through gristle at the left side of the parson's nose. Take it behind the parson's nose and tie ends together.

SPATCHCOCKING A POUSSIN

This technique is applied to poussins and small game birds. The bird is split and flattened so that it can be grilled, barbecued or baked quickly and evenly.

1. Using poultry shears, cut down one side of the backbone.

2. Cut down the other side of the backbone, then remove it. Snip the wishbone in half.

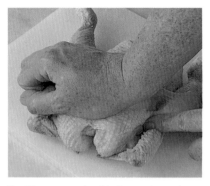

3. Open out the bird on a board and press down hard on the breast bone with the heel of your hand to break it and flatten the bird.

4. Thread two wooden or metal skewers crosswise through each bird to hold it in a flat position. Each skewer passes through a wing and out through the leg on the opposite side.

JOINTING AND BONING POULTRY

All chickens and turkeys are treated in much the same way; size being the only difference. Poussins and spring chickens are best left to your butcher to bone as they're fiddly. A sharp boning knife is essential.

JOINTING

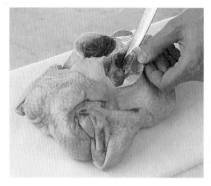

1. Put the bird breast side down and with the tip of a knife cut round the two portions of oyster meat (which lie against the backbone).

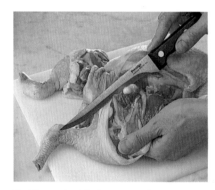

2. Turn the bird over and cut through the skin where the thigh joins the body. Cut right down between the ball and socket joint, being careful to keep the oyster meat attached to the leg. Repeat with the other leg.

3. If liked, separate thighs from drumsticks by cutting through at joints. Trim off bone end from drumsticks.

4. Turn chicken over again, breast down, and cut firmly through the back into the body cavity between backbone and one shoulder blade, leaving wing attached to breast.

5. Repeat on the other side. Then cut right the way through the ribcage, parallel to the backbone on both sides. Pull the back section away.

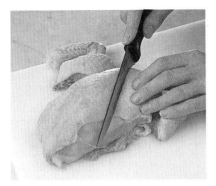

6. Turn the breast with the wings still attached, skin side up. Remove the wing portions by cutting through at a slight diagonal so that some of the breast is attached to the wing. Cut the breast into two or four portions.

BONING WHOLE BIRDS
Choose a bird with a skin that's intact. A good sharp boning knife is essential. This method is applied to turkeys, chickens and ducks.

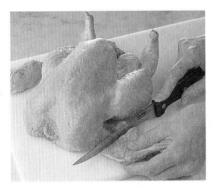

1. Remove the giblets if necessary. Cut off the wings at the second joint. Remove the parson's nose. Cut out the wishbone.

2. Lay the bird breast side down and cut straight down the middle to the backbone. Carefully pull and cut the flesh away from the carcass on each side of the cut until you get to the joints.

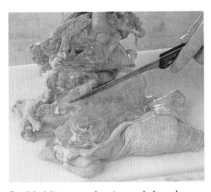

3. Holding one leg in each hand, press firmly outwards to release the ball and socket joints. Cut through the tendons and scrape the meat back from the bone. Pull out the bone, using the knife to help free it as you pull.

4. Cut through the ball and socket joints connecting the wings. Holding the outside of the wing bone in one hand, cut through the tendons and scrape the meat from the bone. Pull the bone free.

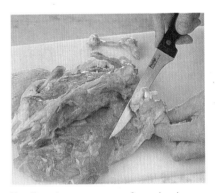

5. Cut the meat away from both sides of the breast until you reach the point where the skin and bones meet without any flesh in between. Being very careful not to puncture the skin, pull the carcass away (you may have to use the knife to help you but take care as the skin is very delicate).

Hot and Sour Soup

Look out for packs of Thai mixed spices alongside the fresh herbs in larger supermarkets. Each pack usually contains a piece of lemon grass, some kaffir lime leaves, a couple of hot chillies and a few pieces of kuchai (garlic chives). If packs are unavailable, buy spices individually – try oriental food stores. You may find kaffir lime leaves more difficult to track down, but their unique flavour and aroma make them well worth searching for. Traditionally, these pungent flavourings are not removed before serving – but they are not meant to be eaten.

SERVES 4

1 packet fresh Thai mixed
  spices
2 garlic cloves
2.5 cm (1 inch) piece fresh
  root ginger
handful of fresh coriander
  sprigs
1.2 litres (2 pints) good
  chicken stock
1 chicken breast fillet,
  skinned
125 g (4 oz) mushrooms,
  preferably shiitake or
  baby button mushrooms
juice of 2 limes
about 30 ml (2 tbsp) light
  soy sauce
1-2 spring onions, to garnish

PREPARATION TIME
15 minutes
COOKING TIME
25 minutes
FREEZING
Not suitable

50 CALS PER SERVING

1. To prepare the herbs, crush the lemon grass using a rolling pin. Slice 1 or 2 chillies (retaining the seeds), depending on how hot you like your soup, but it should be fairly hot. Peel the garlic and thinly slice. Thinly slice the unpeeled ginger. Put all the Thai herbs in a large saucepan with half the coriander and the stock. Cover and bring to the boil.

2. Meanwhile, cut the chicken into strips and halve or slice any larger mushrooms. When the stock has come to the boil, reduce the heat so that it is just simmering. Drop the chicken and mushrooms into the soup. Cover and simmer gently for 20 minutes.

3. Meanwhile, make the garnish. Trim the spring onions and cut into 7.5 cm (3 inch) lengths. Halve each piece lengthways, then cut into very fine shreds. Drop them into a bowl of cold water and leave in the refrigerator to curl. (This garnish is not essential; if you're short of time you could simply trim the spring onions and cut into thin slices on the diagonal.)

4. Check that the chicken is cooked. Add the lime juice and soy sauce to the soup, then taste. The flavour should be fairly hot and faintly sour. If it needs more salt, add a little extra soy sauce. Add more chilli if necessary. Remove and discard the coriander sprigs.

5. Drain the curled spring onion shreds. Ladle the soup into warmed individual bowls and top each with a pile of onion shreds and fresh coriander sprigs.

NOTE: For a more substantial soup to serve as a lunch or light supper, add some fine egg noodles 5 minutes before the end of the cooking time.

VARIATION

Replace the chicken with 225 g (8 oz) peeled raw prawns. Simmer the soup with the mushrooms for 20 minutes before adding the prawns. Add the prawns and simmer gently for 4-5 minutes or until the prawns are cooked through (they will look pink and opaque).

TECHNIQUE

Bruise the lemon grass stalk by striking it firmly with the end of the rolling pin to release the flavour.

CHICKEN LIVER CROSTINI

Try to use a thin 'French-style' baguette for making the bread croûtes. The larger, fatter versions are rather cumbersome, too crusty and open textured. If you can't get hold of a baguette, use slices of white bread cut into neat triangles. And don't try to use margarine for frying; butter is essential for the unmistakable croûton flavour. To serve this as a light main course, top each portion with a couple of slices of Parma ham.

SERVES 4-6

450 g (1 lb) chicken livers
½ baguette
50-75 g (2-3 oz) butter
1-2 large garlic cloves
50 g (2 oz) French beans,
    mangetouts or sugar snap
    peas
selection of salad leaves,
    such as batavia, oakleaf
    lettuce and radicchio
15 ml (1 tbsp) wholegrain
    mustard
45 ml (3 tbsp) raspberry or
    garlic vinegar
75 ml (5 tbsp) olive oil
salt and pepper
chopped fresh parsley, to
    garnish

PREPARATION TIME
20 minutes
COOKING TIME
5 minutes
FREEZING
Not suitable

550-365 CALS PER SERVING

1. Trim the chicken livers and remove and discard any membranes and the white fibrous bit in the middle. Cut each one into 3 or 4 pieces and set aside.

2. Cut 12 thin slices from the baguette, on the diagonal. Heat 50 g (2 oz) butter in a frying pan and fry the bread in batches on both sides until golden brown and crisp, adding more butter to the pan if necessary. Remove from the pan and drain on crumpled kitchen paper.

3. Peel the garlic and cut in half. Rub over both sides of the bread to flavour it with a hint of garlic. If you like a pronounced garlic flavour, repeat this process with a second clove.

4. Trim the French beans, mangetouts or sugar snap peas, then drop into a pan of boiling salted water. Cook French beans for 2 minutes; mangetouts for 30 seconds; sugar snap peas for 1 minute. Drain and refresh with plenty of cold water; drain thoroughly.

5. Arrange the salad leaves on individual serving plates and scatter the blanched vegetables on top.

6. In a bowl, whisk together the mustard, 15 ml (1 tbsp) of the vinegar and 60 ml (4 tbsp) of the olive oil. Season with salt and pepper. Pour this dressing over the salad leaves and carefully toss

each portion to coat all the leaves. Position 3 croûtes on each portion of dressed salad leaves.

7. Add the remaining olive oil to any butter left in the frying pan and heat. Add the chicken livers and cook swiftly over a high heat for 3 or 4 minutes; they should be brown on the outside but still pink in the centre. Using a slotted spoon, remove the cooked livers from the pan and pile on top of the croûtes.

8. Quickly add the remaining vinegar to the pan and heat gently, scraping up any sediment on the bottom of the pan. Season with salt and pepper to taste, then pour over the chicken livers. Scatter with plenty of chopped parsley and serve immediately.

TECHNIQUE

Trim away any membranes and tubes from the chicken livers before cutting them into smaller pieces.

CHICKEN LIVER AND PISTACHIO PÂTÉ

This tasty pâté is blended with cream cheese rather than butter to give a lighter, less calorific result. If you are concerned about calories you could omit the butter seal altogether and instead decorate it simply with chopped herbs. As a starter which can be prepared well ahead and doesn't require last minute titivation, it is ideal if you are entertaining. If you haven't enough suitable individual dishes, set it in one large serving dish.

SERVES 8-10

2 rashers of streaky bacon,
    derinded
700 g (1½ lb) chicken livers
1-2 garlic cloves
about 225 g (8 oz) butter
large pinch of ground
    allspice
125 g (4 oz) flat
    mushrooms
1 medium onion, peeled
200 g (7 oz) low-fat soft
    cheese
30 ml (2 tbsp) double cream
40 g (1½ oz) shelled
    pistachio nuts
45 ml (3 tbsp) chopped
    mixed fresh parsley,
    chives and thyme
salt and pepper
TO GARNISH
parsley or other herb leaves
few shelled pistachio nuts

PREPARATION TIME
20 minutes, plus overnight
chilling
COOKING TIME
15 minutes
FREEZING
Suitable

435-350 CALS PER SERVING

1. Chop the bacon finely. Place in a heavy-based frying pan and heat gently until the fat starts to run, then increase the heat and cook until lightly browned.

2. Meanwhile, trim the chicken livers and remove any membranes and the white fibrous bits in the middle. Roughly chop the livers. Peel and chop the garlic.

3. Add 50 g (2 oz) of the butter to the pan and heat until just melted. Add the livers to the pan with the garlic and all-spice, and cook briskly over a high heat until the livers are sealed and browned on the outside but still a little pink (but not bloody) on the inside. Remove the bacon and livers from the pan with a slotted spoon and set aside.

4. Finely chop mushrooms and onion. Add to the pan and cook gently until the onion is softened. Remove from the heat.

5. Transfer the livers and bacon to a blender or food processor. Add the onion and mushrooms, along with any butter remaining in the pan. Add the soft cheese and cream and work until smooth. Turn into a mixing bowl.

6. Roughly chop the nuts and herbs, then fold into the pâté. Season with salt and

pepper to taste. Spoon the pâté into small individual dishes and level the tops.

7. Melt the remaining butter in a small saucepan over a very low heat. Slowly pour into a jug, leaving the milky sediment behind. Slowly pour the clarified butter onto the pâtés to cover them completely. (Depending on the size of your dishes you may need to melt a little more.) Immerse herbs and pistachios in the butter to garnish. Chill overnight to set. Serve with plenty of good bread or toast.

VARIATION

To make a milder pâté, increase the cream cheese to 400 g (14 oz).

TECHNIQUE

Slowly and carefully pour the melted butter into a measuring jug, leaving the milky sediment behind.

ASPARAGUS AND CHICKEN SALAD

A heavy-based ridged frying pan or griddle greatly enhances the appearance of this dish – applying golden brown stripes across the chicken. Don't despair if you lack such sophisticated equipment in your kitchen – it will taste just as good if you use an ordinary frying pan!

SERVES 4

2 sun-dried tomatoes

15 ml (1 tbsp) capers

about 8 stoned black olives

1 small garlic clove, peeled

about 120 ml (8 tbsp) virgin
   olive oil

20 ml (1½ tbsp) red or
   white wine vinegar

salt and pepper

large pinch of sugar

2 large chicken breast fillets,
   skinned

225 g (8 oz) thin asparagus

TO SERVE

chopped basil or parsley
   (optional)

small piece of fresh
   Parmesan cheese

PREPARATION TIME
15 minutes
COOKING TIME
10 minutes
FREEZING
Not suitable

420 CALS PER SERVING

1. To make the dressing, finely chop the sun-dried tomatoes, capers, olives and garlic. Whisk 105 ml (7 tbsp) of the olive oil with the wine vinegar to make a thick dressing. Stir in the chopped ingredients with the sugar, and season to taste with pepper and a little salt.

2. Beat the chicken breasts between two sheets of cling film to flatten thoroughly. Heat a heavy-based ridged frying pan or griddle pan and brush with olive oil. Cook the chicken for 3-4 minutes on each side until golden on the outside and cooked right through. Cut into neat serving pieces and set aside.

3. Meanwhile, trim the asparagus and peel the woody ends. Tie it in a bundle with string. Bring a 7.5 cm (3 inch) depth of salted water to the boil in a small pan. Stand the bundle of asparagus in the pan, tips uppermost, and cover with a piece of foil. Cook for 5 minutes or until the asparagus is just tender but still retaining some bite. Drain thoroughly and set aside.

4. Arrange the asparagus and chicken on individual plates. Pour on the dressing and sprinkle with herbs, if desired. Using a swivel peeler, shave fine slivers of Parmesan and scatter over the salads. Serve while still warm, or cold.

VARIATION

Replace the asparagus with courgettes, sliced lengthways. To save time, substitute precooked or smoked chicken for the chicken breasts.

TECHNIQUE

Stand the bundle of asparagus in the pan of boiling salted water with the tips uppermost.

CHICKEN AND LEEK TART

Here's a foolproof pastry that's quick to put together and a delight to handle! What's more – providing you cook it in a metal flan tin – it will be crisp on the bottom even though it isn't baked blind. When buying leeks don't forget to allow extra for wastage. You may find that as much as a third of the weight is lost after trimming.

SERVES 8

PASTRY
225 g (8 oz) plain white flour
salt and pepper
1 egg
45 ml (3 tbsp) olive oil
FILLING
700 g (1½ lb) trimmed leeks
25 g (1 oz) butter
15 ml (1 tbsp) olive oil
75 g (3 oz) Gruyère cheese,
finely grated
150 ml (¼ pint) double or
soured cream
2 eggs
freshly grated nutmeg
300 g (10 oz) cooked
chicken
TO SERVE
handful of rocket or dark
green lettuce leaves
Parmesan shavings
paprika, for sprinkling

PREPARATION TIME
1 hour
COOKING TIME
30 minutes
FREEZING
Suitable

410 CALS PER SERVING

1. To make the pastry, put the flour, salt and pepper in a bowl and make a well in the centre. Beat the egg with the olive oil, then pour into the well. Add 45 ml (3 tbsp) warm water and mix to a soft, smooth dough, adding a little extra water if necessary.

2. Briefly knead the dough in the bowl, then wrap in cling film. Leave to rest at room temperature while making filling.

3. To make filling, slit leeks lengthwise and wash thoroughly under cold running water. Shake dry, then slice thinly.

4. Heat the butter and oil in a large heavy-based saucepan, add the leeks and cook over a fairly high heat for about 5 minutes or until slightly softened. Lower the heat, cover with a tight-fitting lid and cook for about 30 minutes or until the leeks are really soft. Don't keep lifting the pan lid as they cook – it will let precious steam escape and the leeks will be more likely to stick; instead gently shake the pan from time to time.

5. Meanwhile, roll out the pastry on a lightly floured surface and use to line a greased shallow 25 cm (10 inch) loose-based flan tin. Cover and chill in the refrigerator while completing the filling.

6. Cut the chicken into thin strips. Pre-heat the oven to 200°C (400°F) Mark 6.

7. When the leeks are cooked to a soft green mush remove from the heat, then add the Gruyère cheese, cream and lastly the eggs. Mix thoroughly and season with salt, pepper and nutmeg to taste.

8. Arrange the chicken in the pastry case and spoon the leek mixture on top. Put the tart on a baking sheet and bake in the oven for about 30 minutes or until just set in the middle and golden brown.

9. Meanwhile finely shred the rocket or lettuce.

10. Leave the flan in the tin for 10 minutes, then remove and cut into wedges. Arrange on individual serving plates and scatter the shredded greenery and Parmesan shavings on top. Sprinkle with a little paprika and serve immediately.

TECHNIQUE

Line a shallow fluted 25 cm (10 inch) loose-based flan tin with the pastry, pressing it gently against side of tin.

DUCK SALAD WITH PEPPER AND ORANGE RELISH

I tend to make this relish with a large red chilli from a home-dried batch so I know its strength – fierce! My guests like it with plenty of zing but, if you're feeding people you don't know so well or using chillies that are unfamiliar, it's best to proceed with caution. Add half at first, taste halfway through, then add more if you think you'll get away with it! Whatever you do, don't forget to remove the chilli before serving. . .

SERVES 4

2 large onions
2 large red peppers
about 60 ml (4 tbsp) virgin
    olive oil
finely grated rind and juice
    of 1 medium orange
½-1 dried chilli
20 ml (1½ tbsp) sugar
15 ml (1 tbsp) orange
    marmalade
15 ml (1 tbsp) wholegrain
    mustard
4 generous handfuls of
    rocket
2 duck breast fillets, each
    about 225 g (8 oz)
salt and pepper

PREPARATION TIME
10 minutes
COOKING TIME
1 hour 20 minutes
FREEZING
Suitable: relish only

540 CALS PER SERVING

1. Peel, halve and slice the onions. Halve and core the peppers, then remove the seeds. Cut the flesh into strips. Heat 15 ml (1 tbsp) olive oil in a heavy-based saucepan, add the onions and peppers and cook over a high heat for 5 minutes until beginning to soften.

2. Add the orange rind and juice, the chilli and sugar. Lower the heat, cover and simmer very gently for about 1 hour or until the vegetables are really soft and the onion is caramelised. Remove the lid from the pan and cook over a high heat for 1-2 minutes to evaporate excess moisture. Remove the chilli and discard. Add the marmalade and mustard and season to taste with salt and pepper.

3. Preheat the oven to 230°C (450°F) Mark 8. Heat 15 ml (1 tbsp) olive oil in a heavy-based frying pan and thoroughly brown the duck on each side. Transfer to a roasting tin and cook in the oven for 10 minutes.

4. Meanwhile arrange the rocket on individual serving plates and season with salt and a little pepper to taste. When the duck is almost ready, drizzle each portion of rocket leaves with a little olive oil and gently reheat the pepper and orange relish.

5. Carve the duck into wafer-thin slices. Arrange on top of the rocket. Top each portion with a spoonful of the pepper and orange relish and serve immediately.

VARIATIONS

If you don't like the strong flavour of rocket, serve the duck breasts on a bed of mixed leaves. Look out for packets of ready-prepared salad leaves in supermarkets. Failing that, a good crisp cos lettuce torn into large pieces works well. The relish is also delicious with sausages and barbecued chicken.

TECHNIQUE

Brown the duckling breasts on both sides, skin-side down first.

DUCK RILETTES

Based on a traditional French method of preserving pork, this makes a really tasty old-fashioned dish. It's not one to go for if you're watching your weight since the meat must be immersed completely in fat. Duck fat or dripping is best for flavour, but not always to hand. Lard is another option, but many find it unpalatable so I tend to use butter. Serve with mustard and plenty of good, crusty bread.

SERVES 4

4 duck leg portions

225 g (8 oz) belly of pork or streaky bacon

2.5 ml (½ tsp) ground allspice

I cinnamon stick

I garlic clove, peeled

freshly grated nutmeg, to taste

salt and pepper

I bouquet garni

a little extra duck fat, butter, dripping or lard (see right)

bay leaves, to garnish (optional)

PREPARATION TIME
15 minutes, plus overnight chilling
COOKING TIME
4 hours
FREEZING
Suitable

460 CALS PER SERVING

I. Using a large heavy knife, cut each duck portion into 2 pieces right through the bone. Remove the rind and any bones from the pork and cut into small pieces. If using bacon, cut each slice into three.

2. Put the meats in a wide heavy-based pan and add all the other ingredients, except the extra duck fat, butter, dripping or lard. Add enough cold water to cover. Bring to the boil, then lower the heat, cover with a tight-fitting lid and simmer very gently for about 4 hours. Check the pan from time to time and add a little more water as necessary to prevent the meat from sticking and burning.

3. After 4 hours, take out a piece of duck and test with a fork. It should be really tender and easy to pull apart in fine threads. If it isn't, cook for a further 30 minutes, then test again.

4. Put a large sieve over a bowl and tip the contents of the pan into the sieve. Leave the liquid to cool, undisturbed.

5. Remove and discard any skin and bones from the duck. Using two forks, pull the meat into threads; do the same with the pork. Discard the bouquet garni, garlic and cinnamon stick. Taste a little of the meat and season with more salt and pepper if necessary.

6. Pack the meat into individual stoneware pots or a large serving pot and top with a few bay leaves if desired.

7. Carefully skim off the solidified fat from the top of the cold cooking liquid and put it into a pan. Heat gently until melted, then pour over the potted meat to cover completely. If there is not enough, melt some extra fat of your choice and use to complete the seal. Sprinkle with pepper.

8. Chill overnight before serving, with crusty wholemeal or French bread.

TECHNIQUE

Using two forks, separate the tender duck meat into fine threads.

NORMANDY CHICKEN FRICASSÉE

A rich creamy casserole flavoured with cider, bay and crème fraîche served with golden sautéed apples. Choose small crisp eating apples with plenty of flavour – Cox's orange pippins, Russets and Braeburn are all good. I prefer to serve this on its own and follow it with a salad. If you feel it needs accompaniments, stick to simple boiled potatoes and a crisp green salad tossed with a good sharp vinaigrette.

SERVES 8

2 large chickens or 8 large
 chicken quarters
45 ml (3 tbsp) white flour
salt and pepper
450 g (1 lb) button onions
225 g (8 oz) smoked bacon,
 derinded
75 g (3 oz) butter
45 ml (3 tbsp) olive oil
300 ml (½ pint) dry cider
300 ml (½ pint) chicken
 stock
2 bay leaves
8 small eating apples
450 g (1 lb) small open cup
 mushrooms
15 ml (1 tbsp) Dijon
 mustard
150 ml (¼ pint) crème
 fraîche
chopped parsley, to garnish

PREPARATION TIME
40 minutes
COOKING TIME
45-50 minutes
FREEZING
Not suitable

480 CALS PER SERVING

1. Joint the chickens following the instructions on page 8. Alternatively, cut each chicken quarter in half. Toss the chicken pieces in the seasoned flour to coat on all sides.

2. Put the onions in a bowl, pour over enough boiling water to cover and leave to soak for a few minutes; this softens the skins and makes them easier to peel. Drain off the water and peel carefully, leaving the root end attached so they will keep their shape during cooking. Roughly chop the bacon.

3. Heat half of the butter in a large flame-proof casserole dish. Add the bacon and onions and cook until golden brown. Remove from the pan with a slotted spoon and set aside. Add the oil to the pan, increase the heat, then brown the chicken in batches on all sides.

4. Return all the browned chicken pieces to the casserole dish along with any excess flour. Add the cider, stock, bay leaves and seasoning and bring to the boil. Stir to loosen any sediment from the bottom of the pan, then lower the heat, cover and simmer gently for 25 minutes.

5. Meanwhile, core the apples and peel them if preferred. Heat the remaining butter in a heavy-based frying pan. Add the apples and cook until golden brown on the outside, shaking the pan occasionally to ensure that they brown evenly. Lower the heat, add 30 ml (2 tbsp) water, then cover the pan with foil and cook very gently for about 10 minutes or until the apples are cooked but not soft and collapsed.

6. Add the bacon, onions and mushrooms to the chicken. Re-cover and cook for a further 15-20 minutes or until the chicken is cooked right through. Skim off excess fat. Stir in the mustard, crème fraîche and salt and pepper. Serve the fricassée with the apples, sprinkled generously with chopped parsley.

TECHNIQUE

Soak the button onions in boiling water to soften the skins, then peel leaving the root end intact.

SESAME CHICKEN PIES

These tasty parcels can be prepared well ahead and popped into the oven to cook as your guests start eating their first course. Serve with moist accompaniments that can be prepared in advance – such as braised red cabbage, ratatouille or puréed carrots and gratin dauphinoise. Alternatively, if you are short of time, simply serve with a generous mixed salad tossed with a smoked bacon dressing.

SERVES 8

SESAME PASTRY

450 g (1 lb) self-raising white flour

10 ml (2 tsp) salt

30 ml (2 tbsp) mixed chopped fresh herbs, such as parsley, chives and dill or tarragon

50 g (2 oz) sesame seeds

175 g (6 oz) butter or margarine

150 ml (¼ pint) Greek-style yogurt

1 egg, beaten

30-45 ml (2-3 tbsp) milk

FILLING

30 ml (2 tbsp) vegetable oil

8 chicken breast fillets, skinned

about 75 g (3 oz) baby spinach leaves

125 g (4 oz) cream cheese with garlic and herbs

2 egg yolks, beaten, to glaze

PREPARATION TIME
35 minutes
COOKING TIME
30-35 minutes
FREEZING
Not suitable

680 CALS PER SERVING

1. To make the pastry, in a bowl mix together the flour, salt, herbs and sesame seeds. Make a well in the centre. Melt the butter or margarine and pour into the well. Add the yogurt, egg and milk. Beat together to form a soft dough. Briefly knead the dough in the bowl until it is smooth and comes together in a ball. Wrap in cling film and leave to rest at room temperature. Preheat the oven to 200°C (400°F) Mark 6.

2. For the filling, heat the oil in a heavy-based frying pan and briefly cook the chicken breasts in batches on both sides to seal and brown them. Leave to cool. Meanwhile thoroughly wash and trim the spinach, if necessary.

3. Divide the pastry in half. Cut one half into 8 equal pieces. On a lightly floured surface, roll out each piece to an oval, slightly larger than each chicken breast.

4. Lay a chicken breast on each pastry oval. Spread one eighth of the cream cheese on each piece of chicken. Put a generous mound of spinach leaves on top, remembering that it will shrink dramatically when cooked. Season with salt and pepper.

5. Roll out the remaining pastry and cut out 8 ovals slightly larger than the previous ones, to allow for these pastry lids to hang down over the chicken and the filling.

6. Brush the pastry edges with a little egg yolk, then position the pastry lids and press the edges together to seal. Trim the edges to neaten. Brush with egg yolk to glaze and mark a spiral pattern on each pastry lid, using the prongs of a fork. Make a small hole in each parcel to let the steam escape. Transfer to baking sheets and brush with more glaze to ensure that you get a good shine on the finished pastry.

7. Bake in the preheated oven for 30-35 minutes or until golden brown and the chicken is cooked right through. To test if the chicken is cooked, carefully remove one parcel from the baking sheet, turn it upside down and make a small cut through the pastry to the middle of the chicken. The juices should run clear. If there is any trace of pink, return them to the oven for a further 5 minutes. Serve at once.

TECHNIQUE

Pile the spinach leaves on top of the cream cheese covered chicken.

CHICKEN BREASTS STUFFED WITH MUSHROOMS

This is a good choice if you often get into a last-minute panic when entertaining. The chicken breasts can be stuffed in advance, ready to put in the oven once your guests are tucking into their starter. The herb butter can be prepared 1-2 days ahead. Serve with baked herb-topped tomatoes and grilled peppers, or a green vegetable.

SERVES 6

1 shallot
30 ml (2 tbsp) olive oil
125 g (4 oz) small open cup
   mushrooms
40 g (1½ oz) mild creamy
   goat's cheese
2 thin slices of Parma ham
45 ml (3 tbsp) chopped fresh
   parsley
salt and pepper
125 g (4 oz) butter
30 ml (2 tbsp) chopped fresh
   basil
squeeze of lemon juice
6 chicken breast fillets, with
   skin

PREPARATION TIME
25 minutes
COOKING TIME
25-30 minutes
FREEZING
Suitable: herb butter only

500 CALS PER SERVING

1. Peel and very finely chop the shallot. Heat the oil in a heavy-based frying pan, add the shallot and cook gently until softened but not browned. Meanwhile, finely chop the mushrooms. When the shallots are softened, add the mushrooms to the pan and continue cooking until they are well reduced and softened.

2. Remove the pan from the heat, allow to cool slightly, then add the goat's cheese. Finely chop the Parma ham and add to the mixture with half of the parsley and plenty of salt and pepper. Leave the stuffing to cool completely. Preheat the oven to 200°C (400°F) Mark 6.

3. Meanwhile, make the herb butter. Beat 75 g (3 oz) of the butter until soft, then add the remaining parsley, the basil, lemon juice and salt and pepper. Dollop the butter onto a sheet of greaseproof paper and shape into a small sausage using the paper to help you roll it into a neat even shape. Chill in the refrigerator until firm.

4. When the stuffing is cold, carefully loosen the skin from each chicken breast, making sure you keep it attached along one long side.

5. Carefully spoon the stuffing under the chicken skin. Tie the chicken into a neat parcel with string, or secure the filling by pushing a fine wooden skewer through the skin. Lay the chicken in a roasting tin, stuffed-side uppermost.

6. Melt the remaining butter and brush over the chicken. Season with salt and pepper. Roast in the oven for 25-30 minutes or until cooked right through.

7. Cut the herb butter into thin slices. Transfer the chicken breasts to warmed serving plates and top with a couple of slices of herb butter. Serve immediately.

TECHNIQUE

Spoon the stuffing under the chicken skin, carefully pushing it in with a teaspoon to ensure there are no gaps.

THAI CHICKEN CURRY

Serve this exotic curry with a mountain of boiled rice to mop up the delicious juices, and plenty of stir-fried green vegetables. As a main course on its own, rather than part of a meal composed of lots of dishes, it will probably only serve 4. Although that's more than one chicken breast each, the delicious sauce encourages over-eating and there's nothing worse than having friends for dinner and feeling that you should have made more!

SERVES 4-6

2 garlic cloves

I medium onion

I lemon grass stalk

2.5 cm (I inch) piece fresh
   root ginger

2 small hot chillies

small handful of fresh
   coriander

5 ml (I tsp) ground
   coriander

grated rind and juice of
   I lime

2 large tomatoes

6 chicken breast fillets,
   skinned

30 ml (2 tbsp) vegetable oil

30 ml (2 tbsp) nam pla (Thai
   fish sauce)

900 ml (1½ pints) thick
   coconut milk

salt and pepper

TO GARNISH

toasted fresh coconut,
   grated

coriander leaves

red chilli slices (optional)

PREPARATION TIME
15 minutes
COOKING TIME
30 minutes
FREEZING
Suitable

775-520 CALS PER SERVING

I. Peel the garlic cloves. Peel and quarter the onion. Halve the lemon grass. Peel the ginger and cut in half. Put these ingredients in a food processor with the chillies, fresh coriander, ground coriander, lime rind and juice. Process until reduced to a chunky paste, adding a couple of spoonful of water if the mixture gets stuck under the blades.

2. Immerse the tomatoes in a bowl of boiling water for 15-30 seconds, then remove, cool slightly and peel away the skins. Roughly chop the tomato flesh. Cut each chicken breast into 3 pieces.

3. Heat the oil in a large heavy-based frying pan or flameproof casserole. Add the spice paste and cook over a fairly high heat for 3-4 minutes, stirring all the time. Add the chicken and cook for about 5 minutes, stirring to coat in the spice mixture.

4. Add the tomatoes, fish sauce and coconut milk. Bring to the boil, then cover and simmer very gently for about 25 minutes or until the chicken is cooked. Season to taste with salt and pepper. Serve garnished with toasted fresh coconut, coriander leaves, and slices of red chilli if desired.

VARIATION

Replace the chicken with 450 g (I lb) large raw prawns. Peel and devein, then simmer in the sauce for 5-10 minutes only, until they look pink and opaque. Don't overcook or they will be tough.

TECHNIQUE

Process the garlic, onion, lemon grass, ginger, chillies, fresh and ground coriander, lime rind and juice to a chunky paste.

CHICKEN WITH LENTILS AND SHALLOTS

Although in general lentils have suffered from a bad press in this country, the tiny green Puy lentil has become a fashionable ingredient. Your local health food shop is likely to be the least expensive source of supply. To make life easier, prepare the shallots or button onions in advance.

SERVES 6

1 onion

1 celery stick

3 rashers smoked streaky
  bacon, derinded

2 garlic cloves

60 ml (4 tbsp) virgin olive oil

6 chicken supremes

225 g (8 oz) lentils de Puy

2 bay leaves

900 ml (1½ pints) chicken
  stock

salt and pepper

450 g (1 lb) shallots or
  button onions

300 ml (½ pint) red wine

15 ml (1 tbsp) Dijon
  mustard

30 ml (2 tbsp) thin honey

10 ml (2 tsp) balsamic or
  red wine vinegar

15 g (½ oz) butter

10 ml (2 tsp) white flour

PREPARATION TIME
20 minutes
COOKING TIME
About 1 hour
FREEZING
Suitable: Shallots only

500 CALS PER SERVING

1. Peel the onion and chop very finely. Trim the celery and chop very finely. Finely chop the bacon. Peel and crush the garlic.

2. Heat half of the olive oil in a large flameproof casserole dish. Add the chicken supremes, skin-side down, and brown on this side only. Remove and set aside.

3. Add the onion, celery, bacon and garlic to the casserole and cook gently until the onion is transparent. Add the lentils, bay leaves and stock, bring to the boil and simmer for 10 minutes. Season with plenty of salt and pepper.

4. Arrange the chicken supremes on top of the lentils, cover the casserole with a tight-fitting lid and cook gently for about 45 minutes until the lentils are tender and the chicken is cooked right through.

5. Meanwhile, put the shallots or button onions in a bowl, pour over enough boiling water to cover and leave to soak for a few minutes. Drain and peel, being careful to leave the root end intact so that the onions hold their shape during cooking.

6. Put the shallots in a saucepan with the wine, mustard, honey and salt and pepper. Bring to the boil, then lower the heat. Cover and simmer very gently for

about 20 minutes or until the onions are tender but still retain their shape, shaking the pan occasionally to prevent them sticking. Add the vinegar.

7. Using a slotted spoon, transfer the cooked chicken to a heated serving platter and surround with the lentils and shallots; keep warm.

8. Blend the butter with the flour to make a beurre manié. Gradually whisk this into the juices in the casserole dish, a piece at a time. Bring to the boil, whisking all the time, and cook for 1-2 minutes until slightly thickened. Check the seasoning. Pour a little sauce over the chicken; serve the remainder separately.

TECHNIQUE

Place the chicken supremes in a single layer on top of the lentil mixture, then cover with a tight-fitting lid.

GUINEA FOWL WITH ROCKET SAUCE AND SPRING VEGETABLES

Rocket or arugula has an unmistakable pungent, peppery flavour and vivid green colour. Buying the quantity needed for this sauce from a supermarket can be expensive as it tends to be sold in small bags at a premium. However, local Greek and Turkish food stores often sell generous bunches of rocket at a fraction of the price.

SERVES 6

75 g (3 oz) butter
30 ml (2 tbsp) olive oil
2 guinea fowl
450 g (1 lb) very small new potatoes, scrubbed clean
2 garlic cloves, peeled
300 ml (½ pint) dry white wine
8 baby leeks, total weight about 125 g (4 oz)
225 g (8 oz) small new carrots
125 g (4 oz) broad beans, skinned
125 g (4 oz) fresh peas
50 g (2 oz) rocket leaves
150 ml (¼ pint) double cream
salt and pepper
chervil, to garnish

PREPARATION TIME
20 minutes
COOKING TIME
1¼-1½ hours
FREEZING
Not suitable

515 CALS PER SERVING

1. Preheat the oven to 200°C (400°F) Mark 6. Heat 50 g (2 oz) of the butter with the oil in a large frying pan and cook the guinea fowl, one at a time, until thoroughly browned on all sides. Arrange the potatoes in the base of a casserole dish and add the garlic. Put the guinea fowl on top. Pour in the wine and 450 ml (¾ pint) water.

2. Cover with a tight-fitting lid and cook in the oven for 45 minutes. Add the leeks, carrots, broad beans and peas. Re-cover the casserole and cook for a further 30-45 minutes or until the guinea fowl are cooked right through and the vegetables are tender.

3. Remove the guinea fowl and vegetables from the casserole and keep warm. Skim off any excess fat from the cooking liquid, then pour into a measuring jug; you should have about 600 ml (1 pint). Make it up to this quantity with wine, stock or water if you haven't got enough.

4. Put the rocket in a food processor with the cooking liquid and cooked garlic cloves and process until smooth. Return the rocket purée to the casserole.

5. Reheat the rocket purée, add the cream and season with salt and pepper to taste. Bring to the boil, then gradually whisk in the remaining butter a little at a time to make a thin, shiny sauce.

6. Carve the guinea fowl and serve each portion with a few vegetables and a little of the sauce poured over.

VARIATIONS

Replace the rocket with sorrel, but halve the quantity. If both sorrel and rocket are unavailable, try making the sauce with watercress. Small chickens could of course, be used instead of guinea fowl.

TECHNIQUE

Gradually whisk the remaining butter into the rocket sauce.

CINNAMON ROAST POUSSIN WITH COUSCOUS

For this recipe you need spatchcocked poussins. This technique is far easier than it looks, providing you have a good pair of poultry shears. Alternatively, you can buy ready-spatchcocked poussins from some supermarkets and butchers. Depending on the size of your poussins and the appetites of your guests allow ½-1 per person.

SERVES 4

250 g (9 oz) couscous

4 small poussins, each about
    400 g (14 oz)

5 ml (1 tsp) ground
    turmeric

5 ml (1 tsp) ground
    cinnamon

125 g (4 oz) butter

salt and pepper

about 60 ml (4 tbsp) thin
    honey

large pinch of saffron
    strands

2 medium onions

1 garlic clove

50 g (2 oz) pistachio nuts

grated rind and juice of
    1 lemon

TO SERVE

chopped parsley or
    coriander, to garnish

lemon wedges

harissa sauce (see note)

PREPARATION TIME
30 minutes
COOKING TIME
50-55 minutes
FREEZING
Not suitable

720 CALS PER SERVING

1. Preheat the oven to 200°C (400°F) Mark 6. Put the couscous in a bowl and pour over 350 ml (12 fl oz) cold water. Leave to soak for about 15 minutes or until all of the water has been absorbed.

2. Meanwhile, spatchcock the poussins following the instructions on page 7. Place, skin-side uppermost, in two roasting tins.

3. Sprinkle the poussins with the turmeric and cinnamon. Melt 40 g (1½ oz) of the butter and brush over the poussins. Season with salt and pepper. Roast in the preheated oven for 20 minutes. Reduce the temperature to 190°C (375°F) Mark 5 and cook for a further 15 minutes. Brush with a little honey and cook for 15-20 minutes more or until cooked right through.

4. While the poussins are cooking, add the saffron to a little boiling water, then mix with the soaked couscous. Spoon into a large muslin-lined metal sieve and steam over a pan of boiling water for about 35 minutes or until the grains are light and fluffy.

5. Meanwhile peel and slice the onions; peel and chop the garlic.

6. When the poussins are cooked, remove them from the roasting tins;

cover with foil and keep warm. Tip all the juices into one pan, place on the hob and add the onions and garlic. Cook quickly over a high heat until browned and softened. Add the nuts, lemon rind and juice and the remaining butter. Add the couscous and mix carefully with a fork. Season with salt and pepper.

7. Pile the couscous onto a large serving platter. Put the poussins on top and scatter with plenty of chopped fresh parsley or coriander. Serve immediately with lemon wedges, and hot Harissa sauce handed separately.

NOTE: Harissa sauce is available in cans from larger supermarkets and delicatessens.

TECHNIQUE

Sprinkle the poussins with turmeric and ground cinnamon, then brush liberally with melted butter.

AROMATIC DUCK CASSEROLE

This combination of aromatic spices, fruits and nuts owes much to the cooking of the Middle East. To complete the theme, serve with a rice or bulgar wheat pilaff and a cucumber salad. Finish the meal with oranges poached in syrup, accompanied by tiny shortbread biscuits dusted with cinnamon and sugar. Round off the evening with strong coffee and rose-scented Turkish delight.

SERVES 6

6 small onions (not button
   onions)

7 cloves

30 ml (2 tbsp) vegetable oil

9 duckling portions or
   6 breast fillets (see note)

6 green cardamom pods

1 large cinnamon stick

5 ml (1 tsp) cumin seeds

2 pieces of star anise

1 green chilli, halved

1.2 litres (2 pints) chicken
   stock

175 g (6 oz) dried apricots

few dried dates (optional)

salt and pepper

about 60 ml (4 tbsp) ground
   almonds

45 ml (3 tbsp) chopped fresh
   coriander (optional)

PREPARATION TIME
10 minutes
COOKING TIME
1¾-2 hours
FREEZING
Suitable

380 CALS PER SERVING

1. Preheat the oven to 180°C (350°F) Mark 4. Peel the onions and cut five in half, leaving the root end intact so that they retain their shape during cooking. Stick the cloves into the remaining onion.

2. Heat the oil in a large flameproof casserole dish and cook the duckling in batches until thoroughly browned all over. Prick the skin with a fork as it cooks to release some of the fat. Remove the duckling from the casserole and set aside. Add the halved onions to the casserole and cook until tinged with brown on the cut side. Remove and set aside with the duckling.

3. Drain off most of the fat from the casserole, then add the cardamoms, cinnamon, cumin seeds and star anise, and cook for 1-2 minutes, stirring all the time, to release their flavour and aroma. Return the duckling and onions to the casserole, then add the halved chilli and chicken stock. Bring to the boil, then cover and cook in the oven for about 1 hour.

4. Add the apricots, and dates if using, and cook for a further 45 minutes to 1 hour, or until the duckling is really tender. Portions may take 15 minutes longer to cook than breast fillets.

5. Skim off any excess fat and stir in enough ground almonds to slightly thicken the juices. Season with salt and pepper to taste and stir in the coriander, if using. Serve with a rice or bulgar wheat pilaff and a cucumber salad.

NOTE: Duckling portions are not very fleshy, so you need to allow nine to serve 6 people. Duckling breasts are much meatier, so one per person is enough.

Star anise is a pretty star-shaped spice with a delicate anise flavour. Although it is generally regarded as a flavouring in Chinese cooking, here it adds an extra dimension to this otherwise Middle Eastern dish. Look out for it in Chinese grocers, or substitute a small pinch of five-spice powder.

TECHNIQUE

Prick the duck skin with a fork as it cooks, to release some of the fat.

BONED STUFFED CHICKEN

This is the kind of recipe that gives you a glowing sense of achievement as the first slice is carved! Boning a chicken is not difficult – especially with the step-by step guide on page 9 – but it cannot be rushed. It's essential that the bird's skin is not pierced, otherwise the stuffing will leak out.

SERVES 10

1 chicken, about 1.6 kg
  (3½ lb), boned (see page 9)
1 small onion
2 garlic cloves
2 small leeks
1 large courgette
125 g (4 oz) butter
50 g (2 oz) long-grain white
  rice
50 g (2 oz) macadamia nuts
  or skinned hazelnuts,
  toasted
1 small eating apple
50 g (2 oz) farmhouse or well-
  flavoured Cheddar cheese
50 g (2 oz) seedless raisins
finely grated rind and juice
  of 1 lemon
75 g (3 oz) fresh white
  breadcrumbs
120 ml (8 tbsp) chopped
  fresh mixed herbs, such as
  parsley, chives and thyme
salt and pepper
1 egg
4-6 large thick slices ham
flat-leaved parsley, to garnish

PREPARATION TIME
1 hour, plus boning and chilling
COOKING TIME
1½-1¾ hours
FREEZING
Not suitable

305 CALS PER SERVING

1. Spread out the boned chicken, flesh side uppermost, on a clean surface and cover with cling film. Using a rolling pin, slightly flatten the thickest areas to give a fairly even thickness all over. Chill in the refrigerator while making the stuffing.

2. Peel and finely chop the onion and garlic. Trim and thinly slice the leeks. Coarsely grate the courgette. Heat half of the butter in a heavy-based pan, add the onion, leeks and garlic and cook, stirring, for 2-3 minutes until beginning to soften. Cover tightly and cook gently for a further 10 minutes or until the leeks are quite soft. Add the courgette and cook for 2 minutes.

3. Meanwhile, cook the rice in a large pan of boiling salted water until just tender. Drain in a sieve and rinse with plenty of boiling water.

4. Mix together the softened vegetables, rice and nuts. Peel the apple and grate the flesh into the mixture. Grate in the cheese too. Add the raisins, lemon rind and juice, with the breadcrumbs and herbs. Season with plenty of salt and pepper. Add just enough beaten egg to bind the stuffing – don't make it too wet.

5. Preheat the oven to 180°C (350°F) Mark 4. Lay the chicken, flesh-side upper-most, on a clean surface and spoon a third of the stuffing down the centre. Lay 2-3 slices of ham on top, overlapping

them slightly to cover the mixture. Repeat with half of the remaining stuffing and the remaining slices of ham. Top with the remaining stuffing.

6. Fold the chicken over the stuffing and sew the edges together to enclose the filling and make a neat shape. Lay it on a double sheet of muslin and roll up the chicken in the muslin, keeping it fairly tight and in a neat shape. Tie the ends with string.

7. Place in a roasting tin and smear the remaining butter on top of the muslin. Roast in the oven for 1½-1¾ hours, basting occasionally. To test, push a skewer right through the middle – the juices should run clear; if at all pink, return to the oven for 15 minutes, then test again.

8. Leave to cool, wrapped in the muslin, then refrigerate overnight. Serve cut into thick slices, garnished with parsley.

TECHNIQUE

Sew the edges of the chicken together, using a needle and fine cotton string.

PROVENÇALE CHICKEN TART

This is a lovely rich, well flavoured tart suitable for a special *al fresco* lunch or picnic. If possible, buy good marinated olives from a delicatessen rather than the briny ones sold in cans in supermarkets. I wouldn't worry about removing the stones – it's fiddly and almost impossible to do without crushing the olives.

SERVES 8

PASTRY
225 g (8 oz) plain white flour
salt and pepper
125 g (4 oz) butter or
  margarine
FILLING
1 large red pepper
1 large green pepper
3 chicken breast fillets,
  skinned
1 garlic clove
30 ml (2 tbsp) olive oil
2 fresh thyme sprigs
2 eggs
450 ml (¾ pint) crème
  fraîche or double cream
25 g (1 oz) Parmesan
  cheese, freshly grated
handful each of black and
  green olives
5 sun-dried tomatoes in oil,
  drained and halved

PREPARATION TIME
25 minutes
COOKING TIME
30 minutes
FREEZING
Not suitable

625 CALS PER SERVING

1. To make the pastry, put the flour and salt and pepper in a bowl. Cut the butter or margarine into small pieces then rub into the flour using your fingertips, until the mixture resembles fine bread-crumbs. Add about 45 ml (3 tbsp) water or enough to mix to a soft dough. Wrap in cling film and leave to rest in the refrigerator for 15 minutes.

2. Meanwhile, halve the peppers and place under a hot grill, skin-side upper-most, until charred. Cover with a cloth and leave until cool enough to handle, then peel off and discard the skins. Remove the cores and seeds. Cut the pepper flesh into thick strips.

3. Roll out the pastry on a lightly floured surface and use to line a 25 cm (10 inch) loose-based flan tin. Chill briefly while completing the filling.

4. Cut the chicken into thin slices. Peel and finely chop the garlic. Heat the oil in a frying pan, then add the chicken, garlic and thyme sprigs. Cook quickly over a high heat, stirring constantly, until the chicken is browned on all sides. Lower the heat and continue cooking for 3-5 minutes until the chicken is cooked right through. Remove from the pan with a slotted spoon and leave to cool. Discard the thyme sprigs.

5. Preheat the oven to 200°C (400°F) Mark 6. Add the eggs, crème fraîche or cream, Parmesan and peppers to the cooled chicken. Mix thoroughly and sea-son with salt and pepper. Spoon into the pastry case. Sprinkle with the olives and halved sun-dried tomatoes.

6. Put the tart on a baking tray and bake in the oven for about 30 minutes or until the tart is golden brown and just set in the middle. Serve warm or cold.

VARIATION

Replace the peppers with 2 large cour-gettes, sliced. Cook them briefly with the chicken.

TECHNIQUE

Sprinkle the olives and sun-dried tomatoes over the filling before baking.

SPICED SAUSAGE AND CHICKEN TERRINE

Serve this spectacular layered terrine as part of a buffet or picnic spread. Alternatively it can be served as a starter – on a bed of salad leaves dressed with a good mustardy vinaigrette. Buy quality bacon for lining the terrine or you will find that the whole thing is swamped with watery juices and unpleasant white deposits.

SERVES 8-12

300 g (10 oz) derinded thin
   smoked streaky bacon
   rashers
1 shallot or small onion
2 garlic cloves
20 ml (1½ tbsp) mild
   paprika
10 ml (2 tsp) cayenne
   pepper
1 small dried chilli,
   crumbled
15 ml (1 tbsp) tomato purée
700 g (1½ lb) pork
   sausagemeat
2 fresh thyme sprigs
salt and pepper
3 small chicken breast fillets
2 canned pimientos
   (½ × 390 g can)

PREPARATION TIME
20 minutes, plus overnight
chilling
COOKING TIME
1½-1¾ hours
FREEZING
Suitable

525-350 CALS PER SERVING

1. Preheat the oven to 180°C (350°F) Mark 4. Stretch the bacon rashers with the flat of the blade of a large cook's knife. Reserve 3 rashers, then use the remainder to line the base and sides of a 1.2 litre (2 pint) terrine or loaf tin. Let the rashers overhang the top edge.

2. Peel and finely chop the shallot or onion and the garlic. Mix together with the paprika, cayenne, crumbled chilli, tomato purée and sausagemeat. Strip the thyme leaves from the stalks and add to the mixture with plenty of black pepper, and salt. Mix thoroughly.

3. Spoon half of the mixture into the bacon-lined terrine and level the surface.

4. Halve each chicken breast horizontally. Arrange in a layer over the sausage mixture. Season with salt and pepper.

5. Thoroughly drain the pimientos and pat dry with kitchen paper. Arrange a layer of these on top of the chicken. Spoon the remaining sausage mixture on top and level the surface.

6. Lay the reserved bacon rashers on top then fold the overhanging bacon rashers up over these slices to cover the top completely.

7. Cover the terrine with foil and place in a deep roasting tin. Pour sufficient hot water into the tin to come halfway up the sides of the terrine. Bake in the preheated oven for 1½-1¾ hours or until the juices run clear when the terrine is pierced with a skewer.

8. Remove the terrine from the bain-marie and carefully drain off any liquid. Put a couple of heavy weights on top of the foil covering (2 large cans will do). Leave to cool. When cold, transfer the terrine (with the weights still in position) to the refrigerator. Chill overnight.

9. Turn the terrine out onto a board and cut into slices to serve.

TECHNIQUE

Line the base and sides of the terrine or loaf tin with bacon rashers, allowing them to overhang the sides.

CHICKEN PANINO

A good medium-sized round loaf with a crisp crust is essential for this recipe. The Italian *paglieno* loaf – available from Italian delicatessens, larger supermarkets and specialist bakers – is ideal, but any similar loaf will do. The quantities for the filling ingredients are deliberately vague, as much will depend on the size of your loaf. Do make sure that you pack the filling in well, so that the whole thing holds together when cut. Serve panino as a summer lunch, or as part of a picnic.

SERVES 8

1 large crusty loaf
FILLING
1 large aubergine
salt and pepper
3 large courgettes
chilli, garlic or virgin olive
    oil, for brushing
6 red or orange peppers
2 beef tomatoes, sliced
about 225 g (8 oz) Parma
    ham or thinly sliced
    smoked ham
about 275 g (10 oz) thinly
    sliced cooked chicken
marinated artichokes
    (optional), sliced
few sun-dried tomatoes
    (optional)
few stoned olives (optional)
generous handful of rocket
    or large basil leaves

PREPARATION TIME
40 minutes, plus overnight
chilling
COOKING TIME
10 minutes
FREEZING
Not suitable

300 CALS PER SERVING

1. To prepare the filling, slice the aubergine, sprinkle generously with salt and layer in a colander. Leave for 30 minutes – the salt will draw out the bitter juices and excess water.

2. Meanwhile, thinly slice the courgettes, brush with a little oil and cook under a hot grill for a couple of minutes each side until just tinged with brown and softened but still retaining some bite. Season with salt and pepper and leave to cool.

3. Drain the aubergine slices and rinse thoroughly in cold running water. Pat dry, then brush with a little oil and cook under a hot grill for a few minutes each side until tender. Season with salt and pepper and leave to cool.

4. Cut the peppers in half. Remove the cores and seeds. Arrange cut-side down in a grill pan and cook until the skins are blackened and charred. Cover with a cloth and leave until cool enough to handle, then peel off the skins. Leave to cool completely.

5. Cut a large slice from the rounded top of the bread and set aside. Carefully remove the soft bread from inside the loaf, leaving a 2.5-4 cm (1-1½ inch) shell within the crust. Brush the inside of the loaf with oil.

6. Layer all the filling ingredients into the bread shell, seasoning well and drizzling with a little oil between each layer. Try to arrange the ingredients so as to give a good contrast of colours between the layers.

7. Replace the bread lid. Wrap the whole loaf in foil. Put it in the refrigerator with a weight on top and leave overnight.

8. The next day, unwrap the loaf and cut into wedges, using a serrated knife, to serve.

NOTE: To make your own garlic or chilli oil simply immerse blanched, skinned garlic cloves or whole chillies in good quality oil for at least 2 weeks.

TECHNIQUE

Carefully scoop out the soft bread from inside the loaf, leaving a 2.5-4 cm (1-1½ inch) shell.

CHICKEN WITH LIME AND GINGER MAYONNAISE

If you have enough time it's well worth making your own mayonnaise for this, in which case you will probably want to add less lime juice at stage 6. If you're watching calories, use a good low-fat brand of mayonnaise and a low-fat double cream substitute.

SERVES 6

1 chicken, about 1.6 kg
    (3½ lb)
7.5 cm (3 inch) piece of
    fresh root ginger
1 bouquet garni
300 ml (½ pint) dry white
    wine
3 limes
1 little gem lettuce (or cos
    lettuce heart)
4 spring onions
200 ml (7 fl oz) mayonnaise
150 ml (¼ pint) double
    cream
salt and pepper
2 ripe pears
TO SERVE
mixed salad leaves and
    herbs
lime wedges or slices, to
    garnish

PREPARATION TIME
30 minutes
COOKING TIME
1½ hours
FREEZING
Not suitable

505 CALS PER SERVING

1. Cut a small piece off the ginger and reserve. Crush the remainder with a rolling pin; there's no need to peel it. Put the chicken into a saucepan in which it fits snugly. Add the crushed ginger, bouquet garni, wine and the pared rind and juice of 1 lime. Pour over enough water just to cover the chicken. Cover with a lid, then bring to the boil and simmer gently for about 1½ hours or until the chicken is tender.

2. Skim off any scum. Leave the chicken to cool in the liquid.

3. Remove the chicken from the pan. Strain the liquid into a wide saucepan and boil rapidly until reduced to about 150 ml (¼ pint).

4. Meanwhile, remove the chicken from the carcass, discarding all skin and bone. Cut the meat into large bite-sized pieces.

5. Trim the lettuce and shred it very finely. Trim the spring onions and chop finely. Add both to the reduced liquid and cook for 1 minute or until the lettuce is just wilted and the onions are softened. Transfer to a blender and purée until smooth. Let cool completely.

6. Peel and grate the reserved ginger. Finely grate the rind from the remaining limes. Add the ginger and lime rind to the cooled puréed mixture. Fold in the mayonnaise and cream. Add the juice of 1 lime, or to taste. Season generously with salt and pepper.

7. Pour the dressing over the chicken and toss gently together to coat all the pieces of chicken.

8. Halve the pears and remove the cores. Cut into slices and toss in the juice of the remaining lime to prevent discolouration.

9. Arrange the chicken on a bed of mixed salad leaves. Scatter with the pear slices and garnish with lime. Serve with thin slices of raisin bread or other good crusty bread.

TECHNIQUE

Cut the cored pears into elegant, thin slices along their length.

GRILLED SUMMER SALAD

This colourful salad makes a delicious summer lunch to serve in the garden. It can be prepared and assembled in advance and stored in the refrigerator for 1-2 days. Make sure that you bring it to room temperature before serving otherwise, if it is too cold, some of the flavour will be lost. Be generous with the basil too!

SERVES 6

4 chicken breast fillets,
   skinned
about 175 ml (6 fl oz) olive
   oil
45 ml (3 tbsp) ground
   almonds
2 garlic cloves, crushed
10 ml (2 tsp) mild mustard
10 ml (2 tsp) thin honey
30-45 ml (2-3 tbsp) lemon
   juice
large handful of fresh basil,
   stems removed
salt and pepper
450 g (1 lb) small new
   potatoes, such as Pink Fir
   or Belle de Fonteney
2 red peppers
2 green peppers
2 yellow peppers
2 fennel bulbs, trimmed
   (optional)
125 g (4 oz) green beans or
   mangetouts, trimmed
basil leaves, to garnish

PREPARATION TIME
30 minutes
COOKING TIME
30 minutes
FREEZING
Not suitable

320 CALS PER SERVING

1. Flatten the chicken breasts between cling film, using a rolling pin.

2. Heat a heavy-based ridged frying pan or griddle and brush with a little olive oil. Cook the chicken in batches for about 5 minutes each side until golden brown and cooked through. Remove from the pan; leave to cool.

3. Meanwhile, spread the ground almonds in a foil-lined grill pan and toast under a moderate grill until golden brown, shaking the pan occasionally to brown evenly. Turn into a bowl and leave to cool.

4. Add the garlic, mustard, honey and 15 ml (1 tbsp) lemon juice to the almonds and whisk together with a fork. Gradually add 150 ml (¼ pint) olive oil, whisking all the time. Finely chop the basil leaves and add to the dressing. Add a little more lemon juice to taste. Season with salt and pepper.

5. Cut the chicken into manageable pieces and moisten with a little of the dressing. Leave to marinate in a cool place.

6. Cook the potatoes in salted water for about 15 minutes until just tender. Drain, cool slightly, then while still warm cut into thick slices. Pour over a little of the dressing, toss gently, then leave to cool.

7. Halve, core and deseed the peppers, then place cut-side down in the grill pan. Grill under a high heat until the skins are charred. Cover and leave until cool enough to handle, then peel off the skins. Cut the flesh into slices.

8. If using fennel, cut into wedges and cook in a pan of simmering water for 5-10 minutes until slightly softened. Drain thoroughly, then brush with olive oil and grill under a high heat until tinged with brown and cooked through.

9. Cook the green beans or mangetouts in a pan of boiling salted water for 2 minutes. Drain and refresh under cold running water; drain well.

10. To assemble, toss all the ingredients together with the rest of the dressing. Check the seasoning. Arrange on a platter and scatter with basil leaves.

TECHNIQUE

Flatten each chicken breast between two sheets of cling film, using a rolling pin.

FRENCH ROAST CHICKEN

Roasting the chicken in this way ensures that it is deliciously moist and tender – so it's worth the little extra effort involved. Don't be put off by the amount of garlic – it cooks down to a sweet tasting delicate purée that gives real body to the gravy. This gravy does require giblets which, alas, are missing from most supermarket birds. Instead, search out a good free-range chicken from your butcher or local farm – should you be unsuccessful, make do with chicken or vegetable stock.

SERVES 4

1 roasting chicken, about
  1.4 kg (3 lb), with giblets
1 carrot
1 onion
1 bouquet garni
140 g (4½ oz) butter
2 fresh tarragon sprigs
½ lemon
6 garlic cloves
salt and pepper
10 ml (2 tsp) white flour

PREPARATION TIME
10 minutes
COOKING TIME
About 1¼-1½ hours
FREEZING
Not suitable

470 CALS PER SERVING

1. Preheat the oven to 200°C (400°F) Mark 6. Remove the giblets from the chicken and put them in a saucepan with the carrot, onion, bouquet garni and 600 ml (1 pint) water. Bring to the boil, then cover and simmer for 1 hour while the chicken is cooking.

2. Melt 125 g (4 oz) of the butter. Weigh the chicken and calculate the cooking time, allowing 20 minutes per 450 g (1 lb), plus 20 minutes. Put the tarragon and lemon inside the chicken. Lay the bird on its side in a rack in a roasting tin. Brush the uppermost side with butter. Roast in the oven for 20 minutes of the cooking time.

3. Turn the chicken so that the other side is uppermost, brush with more butter and roast for a further 20 minutes.

4. Turn the chicken again, so that the breast is uppermost. Brush with more butter. Scatter the garlic cloves in the base of the roasting tin. Cook the chicken for the remainder of the cooking time, or until the juices run clear when a thigh is pierced with a skewer.

5. Transfer the chicken to a heated serving dish and leave to rest in a warm place for 10 minutes.

6. To make the gravy, skim off excess fat from the roasting tin. Retrieve the garlic cloves and pop them out of their skins back into the tin; mash with a fork. Strain the giblet stock into the pan and bring to the boil.

7. Beat together the remaining butter and the flour. Whisk this beurre manié, a small piece at a time, into the gravy. Simmer for a few minutes, whisking all the time. Season to taste. Serve the chicken accompanied by the gravy and vegetables of your choice.

VARIATION

Roast whole bulbs of garlic with the chicken, basting occasionally so that they don't burn. Serve as a garnish and encourage guests to scrape out the soft flesh and spread on the chicken.

TECHNIQUE

Pop the tarragon sprigs and lemon half into the cavity of the chicken to impart flavour during roasting.

CHICKEN WITH CASHEWS

Serve this mildly spiced dish with cinnamon-flavoured basmati rice or a mushroom pilaff. For the latter, simply sauté a little chopped onion, a few sliced mushrooms and a little crushed garlic in butter until softened, then add the rice and boiling stock and simmer until tender. Enrich with a knob of butter just before serving.

SERVES 4-6

about 1.4 kg (3 lb) chicken
   pieces, such as thighs and
   drumsticks
2 large onions
3 garlic cloves
2.5 cm (1 inch) piece fresh
   root ginger
50 g (2 oz) cashew nuts
45 ml (3 tbsp) vegetable oil
1 cinnamon stick
15 ml (1 tbsp) coriander
   seeds
10 ml (2 tsp) cumin seeds
4 cardamom pods
150 ml (¼ pint) thick yogurt
45 ml (3 tbsp) chopped fresh
   coriander (optional)
30 ml (2 tbsp) chopped fresh
   mint (optional)
TO SERVE
yogurt
garam masala
chopped coriander and mint
   (optional)

PREPARATION TIME
15 minutes
COOKING TIME
About 50 minutes
FREEZING
Suitable

400-270 CALS PER SERVING

1. Skin the chicken pieces. If there are any large ones, such as breasts, cut into 2 or 3 pieces.

2. Peel and chop the onions. Peel and crush the garlic. Peel the ginger and chop it finely.

3. Put the cashew nuts in a blender or food processor with 150 ml (¼ pint) water and work until smooth.

4. Heat the oil in a large flameproof casserole and add the onions, garlic, ginger and all the spices. Cook over a high heat for 2-3 minutes, stirring all the time. Add the cashew purée and cook for 1-2 minutes. Add the chicken and stir to coat in the spices.

5. Lower the heat, then add the yogurt a spoonful at a time, followed by another 150 ml (¼ pint) water. Season with salt and pepper. Lower the heat, cover and cook gently for about 45 minutes or until the chicken is cooked right through.

6. Add the coriander and mint if using, and check the seasoning. Serve each portion topped with a spoonful of yogurt and sprinkled with garam masala. Scatter with chopped herbs too, if desired.

VARIATIONS

This works equally well with lean tender lamb or raw prawns. The lamb will take a little longer to cook – simply add more water as necessary to prevent it sticking. If using prawns, simmer the sauce for 15 minutes, add the prawns and cook until they look pink and opaque.

TECHNIQUE

Add the chicken pieces to the casserole and turn to coat in the spices and cashew purée.

SOUTHERN FRIED CHICKEN WITH CORN FRITTERS

Although it's hard to resist reaching for the ketchup bottle with fried foods like this, a homemade tomato salsa really is a far superior accompaniment. Of course, you could always have the ketchup as well!

SERVES 4-6

6 allspice berries
10 black peppercorns
1 garlic clove
40 g (1½ oz) white flour
2.5 ml (½ tsp) dried thyme
salt and pepper
8-12 chicken drumsticks,
   skinned
1 egg, beaten
125-175 g (4-6 oz) dried
   breadcrumbs
vegetable oil for deep-frying
SWEETCORN FRITTERS
75 g (3 oz) plain white flour
1 egg
75 ml (3 fl oz) milk
200 g (7 oz) can sweetcorn
2 spring onions, trimmed
TOMATO SALSA
6 ripe juicy tomatoes
1 red onion, peeled
1 spring onion, trimmed
¼ cucumber
a little olive oil
dash of wine vinegar
chopped fresh herbs

PREPARATION TIME
15 minutes
COOKING TIME
20 minutes
FREEZING Not suitable

660-440 CALS PER SERVING

1. First make the tomato salsa. Finely chop the tomatoes, discarding the cores. Finely chop the onions and cucumber and place in a bowl with the tomatoes. Mix together, moistening with a little olive oil and vinegar. Season liberally with salt and pepper. Add chopped herbs to taste.

2. For the chicken, crush the allspice berries and peppercorns together, using a pestle and mortar. Peel and finely chop the garlic. Mix the flour with the allspice mixture, garlic, thyme and plenty of salt.

3. Toss the chicken in the flour mixture to coat evenly.

4. Dip each chicken portion first in the beaten egg, and then in the breadcrumbs, making sure that they are completely coated. Arrange in a single layer on a plate and chill while making the corn fritters.

5. To make the corn fritters, put the flour and a large pinch of salt into a bowl and make a well in the centre. Add the egg and milk and beat thoroughly to make a smooth thick batter. Drain the sweetcorn, then fold into the batter. Finely chop the spring onions and fold in.

6. Heat a little oil in a frying pan and fry a few large spoonfuls of the sweetcorn

batter mixture for 2-3 minutes each side until golden brown and crisp. Drain on kitchen paper, then transfer to a heat-proof plate and keep warm in a hot oven while you cook the remainder. (There should be sufficient to make 12 fritters.)

7. Meanwhile heat the oil for deep-frying in a deep-fat fryer to 170°C (325°F). Fry the chicken, in batches, for about 10 minutes until crisp and golden on the outside and cooked right through. Keep warm with the corn fritters.

8. Serve the chicken and corn fritters as soon as they are all cooked, with the salsa.

NOTE: Flavour the tomato salsa with chives, basil or coriander, as preferred.

TECHNIQUE

Coat the egg-dipped chicken portions with the breadcrumbs, pressing gently with your fingertips to help them adhere to the surface.

HEARTY STEW

This satisfying winter stew relies on a good mix of root vegetables to beef up the chicken flavour. The split lentils thicken the liquid and heighten the robust feel of the dish. If you can, serve it in generous-sized soup plates with good thick slices of sourdough bread.

SERVES 4-6

1 chicken, about 1.4 kg (3 lb),
   or 4 chicken quarters
30 ml (2 tbsp) white flour
salt and pepper
30 ml (2 tbsp) olive oil
2 onions
2 parsnips
2 large carrots
2 large potatoes
125 g (4 oz) split red lentils
2 bay leaves
2 garlic cloves (optional)
425 g (15 oz) can black-eye
   or red kidney beans,
   drained
2 courgettes, sliced
45 ml (3 tbsp) chopped fresh
   parsley
15 ml (1 tbsp) snipped fresh
   chives (optional)

PREPARATION TIME
15-20 minutes
COOKING TIME
About 1 hour
FREEZING
Suitable

580-390 CALS PER SERVING

1. Joint the chicken following the instructions on page 8; if using chicken quarters, cut each in half. Sprinkle the chicken with flour and season with salt and pepper.

2. Heat the oil in a flameproof casserole and cook the chicken in batches until well browned on all sides. Remove from the casserole and set aside.

3. Meanwhile, peel the onions and chop roughly. Peel the parsnips, carrots and potatoes; cut them all into chunks. Add a little extra oil to the casserole if necessary and cook the vegetables until lightly browned.

4. Return the chicken to the casserole and add the lentils, bay leaves, garlic if using, and 900 ml (1½ pints) water. Cover with a tight-fitting lid and simmer gently, stirring occasionally, for 45 minutes or until the chicken is tender and the lentils are soft and mushy.

5. Rinse the kidney beans, drain and add to the casserole with the courgettes. Season to taste with salt and pepper. Cook for a further 15 minutes or until the courgettes are just tender and the beans are heated through. If the sauce is too thin, retrieve a few spoonfuls of vegetables, mash them with a potato masher and return to the stew to thicken it slightly. Sprinkle with the chopped parsley, and chives if using. Serve immediately.

NOTE: Before using canned beans, always tip them into a sieve and rinse thoroughly under cold running water to remove the slimy residue.

VARIATION

Instead of black-eye or red kidney beans add a can of mixed beans. My local supermarket sells a wonderful 'mixed bean salad' – comprising of no less than 11 different beans! Check the label before buying – anything mixed with a dressing or flavouring is unsuitable.

TECHNIQUE

Peel the root vegetables and cut them into even-sized chunks.

CHICKEN PIE

This is equally good made with chicken or turkey, and is ideal for using up Christmas leftovers. If possible, use a piece of home-cooked gammon or ham cut into generous chunks. Alternatively, buy a thick slice of good ham from a delicatessen in preference to the flimsy pre-packed slices. I've also made this successfully with chunks of salami.

SERVES 4-6

700 g (1½ lb) cooked
   chicken or turkey
about 225 g (8 oz) cooked
   gammon or ham
2 leeks
350 g (12 oz) mascarpone or
   other cream cheese
1 egg
5 ml (1 tsp) mustard
45 ml (3 tbsp) chopped fresh
   parsley
5 ml (1 tsp) finely grated
   lemon rind
225 g (8 oz) ready-made
   flaky or puff pastry
salt and pepper
beaten egg, to glaze

PREPARATION TIME
20 minutes
COOKING TIME
30 minutes
FREEZING
Not suitable

860-570 CALS PER SERVING

1. Preheat the oven to 200°C (400°F) Mark 6. Cut the chicken or turkey and the gammon or ham into large chunks. Trim the leeks and cut into 2.5 cm (1 inch) slices. Bring a small saucepan of water to the boil. Add the leeks, bring to the boil again and cook for about 2 minutes or until slightly softened. Drain thoroughly, reserving 45 ml (3 tbsp) of the cooking liquid.

2. Put the mascarpone in a bowl and mix with the reserved cooking liquid. Gradually beat in the egg, then add the mustard, parsley, lemon rind and plenty of salt and pepper. Fold in the chicken or turkey, with the gammon or ham and the leeks. Spoon the mixture into a 1.4 litre (2½ pint) pie dish. If you have a pie funnel, push it down into the middle of the filling to support the pastry.

3. Roll out the pastry on a lightly floured surface and trim to an oval about 5 cm (2 inches) larger than the pie dish. Cut off a 2.5 cm (1 inch) strip from all round the oval and press onto the rim of the pie dish.

4. Brush the pastry rim with a little beaten egg, then position the pastry oval on top to make a lid. Press the edges together to seal then, using a sharp knife, knock up the edges. Make a slit in the middle to let steam escape, allowing the funnel to show through if using.

5. Decorate with leaves cut from the pastry trimmings, if desired. Brush the pastry thoroughly with beaten egg.

6. Stand the pie on a baking sheet. Bake in the preheated oven for about 30 minutes or until the pastry is well risen and dark golden brown. Leave to cool and settle for 15 minutes before cutting.

VARIATION

If you are making this at Christmas and you've any leftover Stilton, omit the mustard and flavour the sauce instead with 25-50 g (1-2 oz) crumbled Stilton.

TECHNIQUE

Roll out the pastry on a lightly floured surface to an oval, about 5 cm (2 inches) larger than the pie all round.

Chicken cooked with an olive paste

Most large supermarkets and delicatessens now stock jars of olive paste. Both black and green varieties are available; you can also buy olive pastes blended with flavouring ingredients such as walnuts and capers. Some brands are very oily – if necessary, drain off a little of the oil from the jar before adding the olive paste to the casserole.

SERVES 4

1 chicken, about 1.4 kg (3 lb),
   or 4 chicken quarters
225 g (8 oz) small onions
   (not button onions)
30 ml (2 tbsp) olive oil
2 garlic cloves, crushed
15 ml (1 tbsp) tomato purée
15 ml (1 tbsp) mild paprika
425 g (15 oz) can chopped
   tomatoes
100 g (3½ oz) jar black olive
   paste
salt and pepper
1 large green pepper
400 g (14 oz) can artichoke
   bottoms or hearts,
   drained and halved
TO GARNISH
basil leaves
few black olives
chopped parsley

PREPARATION TIME
20 minutes
COOKING TIME
About 1 hour

350 CALS PER SERVING

1. Joint the chicken following the instructions on page 8; if using chicken quarters, cut each one in half. Peel the onions and cut into quarters.

2. Heat the olive oil in a flameproof casserole and cook the chicken in batches until thoroughly browned on all sides. Remove the chicken from the casserole and set aside. Add the onions to the casserole and cook, turning occasionally, until tinged with brown.

3. Add the garlic, tomato purée and paprika and cook for 2 minutes, stirring all the time. Add the tomatoes and olive paste; stir to mix thoroughly. Return the chicken to the casserole and season with salt and pepper. Cover, lower the heat and simmer gently for 45 minutes or until the chicken is tender.

4. Meanwhile halve the green pepper and remove the core and seeds. Cut the pepper into very, very thin strips.

5. Add the pepper strips and artichokes to the casserole, re-cover and cook for a further 15 minutes or until the pepper strips are tender and the chicken is cooked right through. Check the seasoning. Serve immediately, garnished with basil, olives and chopped parsley.

TECHNIQUE

Cut the green pepper into fine strips – they should be wafer-thin and certainly no wider than a matchstick.

CHICKEN PISSALADIÈRE

I have to admit to making this with the pre-sliced wafer-thin chicken sold in puffy plastic packs for sandwiches! It doesn't have much texture or real flavour – but young children love it. For a more adult style pissaladière, leftover chicken or turkey gives a far better flavour and texture. Alternatively, buy good quality roast chicken or turkey from a delicatessen.

SERVES 4

280 g (10 oz) packet pizza
    base or white bread mix
30 ml (2 tbsp) olive oil
450 g (1 lb) onions
about 225 g (8 oz) cooked
    chicken or turkey
salt and pepper
50 g (1¾ oz) can anchovy
    fillets
handful of black or green
    olives

PREPARATION TIME
About 40 minutes
COOKING TIME
About 35 minutes
FREEZING
Suitable

485 CALS PER SERVING

1. Oil a large flat baking sheet. Make the dough following the instructions on the packet. Knead for 5 minutes on a lightly floured surface until smooth and elastic.

2. Shape the dough into a ball then place it in the middle of the baking sheet. Roll out or press the dough to a 30 cm (12 inch) circle. Cover loosely with a sheet of oiled cling film and leave in a warm place while making the filling.

3. Peel and slice the onions. Heat the oil in a large saucepan, add the onions and cook very gently for about 30 minutes or until softened but not browned. If they show signs of sticking, add a spoonful of water. Preheat the oven to 200°C (400°F) Mark 6.

4. Arrange the chicken on the bread dough, to within 2.5 cm (1 inch) of the edge. Spoon the onions evenly on top and scatter with the anchovies and olives. Bake in the oven for 35 minutes or until well risen and golden brown. Serve hot, warm or cold.

VARIATION

For a more elaborate pissaladière, top with thin strips of grilled pepper. Simply halve, core and deseed 3 large peppers. Place cut-side down on a baking sheet and grill until the skins are blackened. Cover with a cloth and leave until cool

enough to handle, then peel off the skins and cut the flesh into neat strips. Arrange on top of the pissaladière.

TECHNIQUE

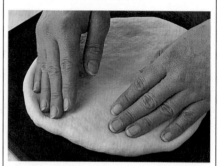

Lightly press the dough out to a 30 cm (12 inch) circle on the oiled baking sheet.

CHICKEN, POTATO AND SPINACH FRITTATA

For this tempting frittata choose waxy potatoes which hold their shape when sautéed. Look for varieties such as Wilja, Belle de Fonteney and Maris Bard. Some supermarkets print information on bags of potatoes or ask your greengrocer if you need advice. Use a good heavy-based frying pan to cook the frittata, or it will stick.

SERVES 4

450 g (1 lb) waxy potatoes

2 onions

225 g (8 oz) cooked chicken
   or turkey

about 60 ml (4 tbsp) olive oil

1 garlic clove, crushed
   (optional)

handful of baby spinach
   leaves or 1 large
   courgette

salt and pepper

freshly grated nutmeg

5 eggs (size 1)

PREPARATION TIME
10 minutes
COOKING TIME
20 minutes
FREEZING
Not suitable

350 CALS PER SERVING

1. Peel the potatoes and cut into 2.5 cm (1 inch) chunks. Peel the onions, cut in half, then slice. Cut the chicken or turkey into bite-sized pieces.

2. Heat half of the oil in a heavy-based, preferably non-stick, frying pan. Add the potatoes, onions and garlic, if using. Cook over a high heat until the vegetables are tinged with brown. Reduce the heat and continue cooking, stirring occasionally, until the potatoes are cooked. If the mixture starts to stick, add a little more oil.

3. When the potatoes are cooked, add the chicken or turkey and cook over a high heat for 5 minutes or until the chicken is heated through. Meanwhile trim the spinach or slice the courgette. Add to the pan and season with salt, pepper and nutmeg. If using courgette, cook for a further 2 minutes to soften.

4. Add a little extra oil to coat the bottom of the pan if necessary. Heat for 1 minute, then add the beaten eggs. Continue cooking over a high heat for about 2 minutes, to set the egg at the bottom, then lower the heat and cook until the egg at the top is just set.

5. Remove the pan from the heat. Using a palette knife, carefully loosen the frittata around the edge. Invert a plate over the pan, then turn the plate and pan over to release the frittata onto the plate. Slide the frittata back into the pan and cook for 1-2 minutes more. Serve immediately, accompanied by a tomato salad and crusty bread.

VARIATION

Add some chopped salami and a handful of olives at stage 3.

TECHNIQUE

Pour the beaten eggs evenly over the ingredients in the pan.

BARBECUE CHICKEN

The crux of this dish is the size of the potatoes – it won't be a quick supper if your potatoes are too large! Look out for ready-washed tiny potatoes, about the size of a large walnut. The recipe works well with baby onions, as they retain their shape when cooked, but they're fiddly and time consuming to prepare, so here I've used sliced onions instead.

SERVES 4

450 g (1 lb) tiny potatoes, scrubbed clean

salt

8 chicken drumsticks, skinned, (or 4 thighs and 4 drumsticks)

2 onions

120 ml (8 tbsp) tomato ketchup

30 ml (2 tbsp) soft dark brown sugar

15 ml (1 tbsp) mild mustard

30 ml (2 tbsp) Worcestershire sauce

1 garlic clove, crushed

15 ml (1 tbsp) vegetable oil

PREPARATION TIME
About 15 minutes
COOKING TIME
40-50 minutes
FREEZING
Not suitable

450 CALS PER SERVING

1. Preheat the oven to 220°C (425°F) Mark 7. Add the potatoes to a saucepan of cold salted water. Bring to the boil, lower the heat and cook for 5 minutes.

2. Meanwhile, make 2-3 deep cuts in each piece of chicken. Peel the onions and cut into fairly thick rings.

3. In a large bowl, mix together the tomato ketchup, sugar, mustard, Worcestershire sauce and garlic. Add the chicken and onions, and stir until well coated with the sauce.

4. Drain the potatoes. Heat the oil in a roasting tin on the hob. Quickly tip the potatoes into the hot oil and shake the tin so that the potatoes are evenly coated with oil.

5. Turn off the heat, then add the chicken and onions, with the sauce. Mix thoroughly, then bake in the preheated oven for 40-50 minutes or until the chicken is cooked right through and the potatoes are tender. Stir occasionally during cooking, to ensure everything browns evenly.

6. Serve accompanied by a crisp leafy salad and some good crusty bread.

VARIATION

Replace half of the chicken portions with spicy sausages.

TECHNIQUE

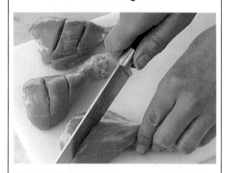

Make 2-3 deep slashes on each chicken piece, using a sharp knife. This allows the barbecue sauce to penetrate and flavour the chicken.

PASTA WITH CHICKEN AND NIÇOISE SAUCE

Although this isn't a traditional Provençale recipe, it has many of the flavours associated with that fertile area — thyme, olives, tomatoes, courgettes and, of course, garlic. If you're making this during the summer and you come across some ripe, red squashy tomatoes use them, rather than opening a can. Flavourless tomatoes simply will not do!

SERVES 4

2 shallots or 1 onion

2 garlic cloves

1 hot red chilli

2 chicken breast fillets, skinned

45 ml (3 tbsp) virgin olive oil

2 fresh thyme sprigs

425 g (15 oz) can chopped tomatoes

generous splash of red wine

2 small courgettes (optional)

about 450-700 g (1-1½ lb) dried pasta ribbons, such as pappardelle or tagliatelle

handful of black and green olives

15 ml (1 tbsp) capers (optional)

salt and pepper

chopped fresh parsley, to garnish

PREPARATION TIME
10 minutes
COOKING TIME
About 20 minutes
FREEZING
Suitable: Sauce only

640 CALS PER SERVING

1. Peel and finely chop the shallots or onion and the garlic. Chop the chilli. Cut the chicken into bite-sized pieces.

2. Heat the olive oil in a large saucepan. Add the chicken and cook over a high heat until browned all over. Remove from the pan and set aside. Add the shallots or onion, garlic and chilli and cook for a few minutes until softened.

3. Return the chicken to the pan and add the thyme, tomatoes and wine. Bring to the boil, lower the heat and simmer for about 15 minutes or until the chicken is cooked right through.

4. Meanwhile, trim and roughly chop the courgettes, if using. Add the pasta to a large pan of boiling salted water and cook, according to the packet instructions, until *al dente* (cooked but still firm to the bite).

5. Add the courgettes and olives to the sauce, with the capers if using. Season with salt and pepper to taste. Simmer for 5 minutes or until the courgettes are just softened but still retain some bite.

6. Drain the pasta thoroughly in a colander. Serve topped with the sauce and garnished with plenty of chopped parsley.

VARIATION

Halve 2 peppers and grill, cut-side down, until the skins are charred. Cover with a cloth and leave to cool slightly, then peel away the skins. Discard the cores and seeds, and cut the flesh into strips. Add to the sauce with the courgettes.

TECHNIQUE

Fry the bite-sized chicken pieces in the hot oil, turning constantly, until evenly browned.

GRILLED CHICKEN WITH PESTO BUTTER

This method of cooking works just as well with other flavoured butters, such as garlic, lemon or *fines herbes* (a sprightly mixture of chervil, tarragon and chives). As a short cut, you could buy ready-prepared garlic butter. Alternatively, if you're trying to reduce the amount of butter in your diet, you could use olive oil instead – simply whisk about 45 ml (3 tbsp) oil with the pesto and brush over the chicken.

SERVES 4

4 chicken breast fillets,
   supremes or quarters,
   with skin
salt and pepper
75 g (3 oz) butter
45 ml (3 tbsp) pesto
lemon juice, for sprinkling

PREPARATION TIME
10 minutes
COOKING TIME
20-30 minutes
FREEZING
Not suitable

370 CALS PER SERVING

I. Make 3-4 deep cuts on each side of the chicken breasts. If using portions, make several cuts all over the skin side. Season with salt and pepper.

2. Beat the butter until softened, then gradually work in the pesto. Spread the skin side of each portion with half of the pesto butter and sprinkle with a little lemon juice.

3. Preheat the grill to hot. Grill the chicken for about 10 minutes, then turn the portions. Spread with the remaining butter and sprinkle with a little more lemon juice. Grill for 10 minutes or until cooked right through. Some portions may take a further 5-10 minutes, depending on shape and size.

4. Serve the grilled chicken at once, with any accumulated pan juices poured over, and vegetables in season.

VARIATION

Make the butter a little more piquant by adding a chopped fresh chilli and 5 ml (1 tsp) mild paprika.

TECHNIQUE

Spread half of the pesto butter evenly over the skin-side of the chicken portions.

GRILLED CHICKEN WITH A SPICED YOGURT CRUST

Yogurt makes a wonderful basis for a marinade, as it tenderises and flavours yet doesn't disappear during cooking. Instead it forms a delicious soft crust which protects the meat from the fierce heat of the grill. Although I hate to admit it, I like this meal best served with oven chips! They may be unhealthy, but they're less effort than the real thing and great comfort food. I buy the thinly cut variety and find they are best cooked for a little longer than suggested on the packet.

SERVES 4

4 **chicken breast fillets, skinned**

15 ml (1 tbsp) **coriander seeds**

5 ml (1 tsp) **ground cumin**

10 ml (2 tsp) **mild curry paste**

1 **garlic clove, crushed**

450 ml (¾ pint) **natural bio yogurt**

salt and pepper

45 ml (3 tbsp) **chopped fresh coriander (optional)**

PREPARATION TIME
10 minutes, plus marinating
COOKING TIME
20 minutes
FREEZING
Not suitable

245 CALS PER SERVING

1. Prick the chicken breasts all over with a fork and flatten them slightly at the same time.

2. Crush the coriander seeds, using a pestle and mortar (or the end of a rolling pin in a strong bowl). Mix with the cumin, curry paste, garlic and yogurt in a large shallow dish. Add seasoning, and the fresh coriander if using.

3. Add the chicken and turn to coat thoroughly coat with the spiced yogurt mixture. Leave to marinate for 30 minutes, or cover and place in the refrigerator overnight.

4. Preheat the grill to high. Grill the chicken, turning occasionally, for about 20 minutes or until cooked through. To see if it is cooked, pierce the thickest part with a fork and check that the juices run clear. Serve right away with a crisp green salad and oven chips.

NOTE: You could use other cuts of chicken, but they will take longer to cook. Skin them first, then slash in several places to enable the heat to penetrate right through to the middle.

VARIATION

For children, use chicken drumsticks and omit the cumin and coriander for a milder flavour.

TECHNIQUE

Turn the chicken breasts in the spiced yogurt mixture, making sure that they are thoroughly coated.

EGG NOODLES WITH CHICKEN AND VEGETABLES

Vary the vegetable content of this dish according to what you have to hand, but aim to keep a good balance of texture, colour and flavour. If supplies of fresh vegetables are limited, canned sliced bamboo shoots or water chestnuts make a good addition. The chicken isn't intended to be the main ingredient in this dish, so one breast fillet will happily serve 2 people.

SERVES 2

1 chicken breast fillet,
   skinned
1 red pepper
4 spring onions, trimmed
2 carrots, peeled
125 g (4 oz) shiitake or
   button mushrooms
2.5 cm (1 inch) piece fresh
   root ginger (optional)
1 garlic clove
250 g (8.8 oz) packet thin
   egg noodles
about 30 ml (2 tbsp)
   vegetable oil
few beansprouts (optional)
45 ml (3 tbsp) hoisin sauce
30 ml (2 tbsp) light soy
   sauce
15 ml (1 tbsp) chilli sauce
TO GARNISH
shredded spring onion
sesame seeds

PREPARATION TIME
10 minutes
COOKING TIME
About 10 minutes
FREEZING
Not suitable

730 CALS PER SERVING

1. Cut the chicken into very thin strips. Halve, core and deseed the pepper, then cut the flesh into thin strips. Cut the spring onions and carrots into similar-sized strips. Halve the mushrooms. Peel the ginger and garlic, then chop finely.

2. Bring a large pan of water to the boil. Add the noodles and cook for 2-3 minutes or according to the packet instructions. Drain thoroughly and toss with a little of the oil to prevent them sticking together; set aside.

3. Heat the remaining oil in a wok or a large frying pan. Add the chicken, ginger and garlic and cook over a very high heat until the chicken is browned on the out-side and cooked right through.

4. Add all the vegetables to the wok or pan and stir-fry over a high heat for a few minutes or until they are just cooked, but still crunchy.

5. Add the hoisin sauce, soy sauce and chilli sauce and stir to mix. Add the noodles and cook for a couple of minutes to heat through. Serve immediately, sprinkled with shredded spring onion and a few sesame seeds.

VARIATION

Replace the chicken with thinly sliced turkey escalopes. Increase the heat of the dish by frying a chopped chilli with the onion and ginger.

TECHNIQUE

Add all the prepared vegetables to the browned chicken in the wok and stir-fry over a high heat until cooked but retaining some bite.

PAN-FRIED DUCK

I recently came across some dried cranberries in my local supermarket and, as they intrigued me, I bought some. I found them to be sweet yet sharp and far nicer than fresh cranberries, so they found their way into this quick sauce. They add a splash of colour and a tartness that complements the rich duck meat perfectly, though the sauce is equally more-ish without them! Deep-fried parsnips make an ideal accompaniment.

SERVES 2

2 duckling breast fillets,
    each about 225 g (8 oz)
30 ml (2 tbsp) vegetable oil
2 garlic cloves
150 ml (¼ pint) dry red
    wine
pared rind and juice of
    1 clementine or tangerine
1 bay leaf
15 ml (1 tbsp) blackcurrant
    jam
30 ml (2 tbsp) dried
    cranberries (optional)
salt and pepper
5 ml (1 tsp) balsamic or red
    wine vinegar
clementine halves, to
    garnish

PREPARATION TIME
5 minutes
COOKING TIME
35 minutes
FREEZING
Not suitable

460 CALS PER SERVING

1. Thoroughly prick the duckling skin with a fork. Heat the oil in a large heavy-based frying pan. Add the duckling breasts, skin-side down, and cook over a very high heat until the skin is thoroughly browned.

2. Turn the duckling over and brown the other side, then lower the heat and cook for about 10 minutes or until cooked but still a little pink in the centre. Remove from the pan and keep warm. Drain off most of the fat from the pan.

3. Peel and thinly slice the garlic. Add to the pan with all the remaining ingredients, except the vinegar. Bring to the boil, lower the heat and simmer gently for 5 minutes. Season with salt and pepper to taste, then add the vinegar.

4. Carve the duckling into slices and arrange on two warmed serving plates. Spoon the sauce over the duck and garnish each plate with a clementine half. Serve immediately.

NOTE: Deep-fried parsnip ribbons are a delicious accompaniment for this dish. Use small parsnips to make these. Peel, then pare lengthwise into long thin slices, using a swivel potato peeler. Deep-fry in batches in hot oil until golden brown and crisp. Drain on kitchen paper and serve at once.

TECHNIQUE

Prick the skin of the duckling breasts all over, using a fork. This helps to release the fat and crisp the skin during cooking.